To all Quebec artisans who have expressed a love for their trade,
thank you for sharing your talent and your values.
You have inspired me in writing this book.

Canadian Cataloguing-in-Publication Data

Foreman, Michèle

Photos: Michèle Foreman
        Except for photos on pages 20 and 24

Translation: Renata Isajlovic and Michèle Foreman

Revision: Vera Roy

Photographs were taken outdoors, without artifice to modify food appearance.

ISBN 2-9808183-5-6

Legal Deposit – Bibliothèque nationale du Québec, 2005
Legal Deposit – National Library of Canada, 2005

Printed in Quebec

Also available in French, from the same author:
        L'histoire savoureuse d'une région Outaouais – 2003
        L'histoire savoureuse d'une région Bas-Saint-Laurent – 2004
        L'histoire savoureuse d'une région Québec – 2004
        L'histoire savoureuse d'une région Chaudière-Appalaches – 2005

www.stellaireediteur.com

TABLE OF CONTENTS

Foreword 7

Preface by Julian Armstrong 9

The Story of the Land 13

Regional Bounty 17

Keepers of Time 21

Backroad Treasures 29

Recipes 57

Backroad Treasures Addresses 114

Recipes Index 116

Sources of Ingredients 118

Restaurants and Inns 119

FOREWORD

Artisans of this magnificent province, I pay homage to you!

I take this opportunity to acknowledge the commitment of the men and women who have embarked on careers that have long connected us to the land and water.

While seeking inspiration in the customs and traditions of old, these artisans have successfully moved towards modern times. As they pass on the values imparted to them by their forebears, they also know how to separate the wheat from the chaff of today. Through their tenacity and daily work, they have imbued farming, fishing and food processing with a meaning that once again connects these activities with nature.

When it comes to their love for their work, food producers, chefs and pastry chefs wear their hearts on their sleeves. Losing track of the hours, they embrace each day, which brings its own joys and disappointments, its successes and failures. And while food producers grow fruit and vegetables, raise animals, harvest fish and shellfish or process foods, it takes the talents of a chef to bring these wonderful products to our plates. Partnerships are forged, with curiosity fuelling the fire—it doesn't get much better than this.

I would like to share with you some of my fondest moments with these regional artisans, who fully appreciate the value of everything their *terroir* has to offer.

The artisans featured here are gracious and generous. Some welcome visitors to their farms and processing facilities and, with great pride, offer a beverage made with berries, sparkling cider, duck *rillettes* or a poultry *terrine*.

Taking a drive along these country roads is a must. Take the time to stop and meet the artisans. Friendly, kind and brimming with talent, they will help you discover the flavours of Quebec!

Joyeuses gourmandises!

Michèle Foreman

PREFACE

It's tucked away down country lanes or along the shores of remote rivers that Quebec's finest gastronomic products are often found.

Michèle Foreman, a journalist with a discriminating palate and the instincts of a detective, has made it her mission to find these specialties at their source. She speaks with the dedicated people who produce them, photographs them and writes tempting accounts of what she finds. Her reporting on Quebec's savoury history is unique in this food-obsessed province and serves the travelling public interested in replicating her trips as well as consumers who want advice on what specialty products to look for in fine food shops.

Culinary tourism is a major consideration for travellers planning their holidays. But where to go to find a region's specialties? What's worth a detour?

The most widely promoted products are sometimes more ordinary than something produced in small quantities in some out-of-the-way location with no advertising other than a handwritten sign at the gate.

An authoritative guide like Michèle is invaluable. When she shares a tip with me about a product she finds remarkable, an impressive new restaurant or a chef making wonderful use of local ingredients, I listen – and plan my travels accordingly.

And even if you're an armchair traveller, her books make for appetizing reading.

Julian Armstrong

Food Editor
The Gazette

THE STORY OF THE LAND

Quebec is Canada's largest province, stretching northwest from the St Lawrence River and Gulf of St Lawrence all the way to Hudson Strait and Hudson Bay, southwest to the Ottawa River, and northeast to Labrador. The Eastern Townships and the Gaspé Peninsula both lie south of the St Lawrence River.

Geographically, Quebec is divided into three main regions: the upper plateaus of the Canadian Shield that cover most of the territory north of the St Lawrence River; the Appalachian Mountains that run south of the St Lawrence River; and the St Lawrence Valley lowlands that lie between the Appalachian Mountains and the Canadian Shield. The regional landscape, which has undergone constant transformation by the elements, has been marked by long glacial periods, with the Champlain Sea flooding the land only to eventually recede, revealing various types of clay, sand and gravel. This fertile agricultural zone was the site of the first European settlements.

French pioneers who made their way up the St Lawrence River settled in the area around Quebec City. After exploring Acadia, Samuel de Champlain travelled up the St Lawrence and stopped in Quebec City in 1608. Twenty-five years later, the Compagnie des Cent-Associés was granted the entire territory stretching from the Arctic Circle to Florida, as well as a permanent fur trade monopoly for the purposes of settling the area.

A 1667 census reveals that the Côte de Beaupré population outnumbered that of Quebec City. The plain stretching along the northern Estuary and the sunny terrace that borders it have always been prized here.

By the late 17th century, all of the land on Île d'Orléans had been claimed.

As early as the 17th century, Quebec City had a surplus of workers and supplied labour to other parts of the colony as it expanded inland. The farms of Guillaume Couillard and Louis Hébert were among the first in New France, with the Côte de Beaupré and Île d'Orléans becoming the agricultural jewels of the Quebec City area.

The Roots of Farming

Wheat was a dietary staple and dominated crops until around 1830. Soil depletion, insects, variable weather conditions and competition from farmers in Upper Canada spelled the beginning of the end of the grain's dominance in Quebec. A more diversified farming system was established, with oats, hay and potato crops increasingly gaining importance. Beginning in the 1870s, milk production was boosted by demand for butter and cheese in Great Britain and the growing urban market. Dairy farming spearheaded agriculture in the 20th century and still accounts for half of all commercial farms in Quebec.

Seigneuries, which were tracts of land originally granted to individuals by the King of France, played an important role, as did Aboriginal peoples, who passed on their traditions to settlers, introducing them to such things as the virtues of maple sap.

While logging fuelled the development of the Outaouais region in the westernmost part of the province, the boom in agriculture is attributable to the consequent need to feed forestry workers.

Subsistence farming grew alongside the forestry industry, eventually becoming a commercial operation to meet the needs of workers for large forestry companies. Mining also sparked demand for agricultural goods.

Farther east, along the banks of the nourishing St Lawrence, there were enough elements, including hunting, fishing, berry growing and harvesting opportunities, to attract settlers. Around 1800, surpluses of eel, grain, cured beef, pork, lard and butter were exported via the St Lawrence River, the first "highway" to major centres.

A number of regions were blessed with many different types of soil, which enabled some farms to diversify their crops.

The slightest advantage in weather could make a big difference. For instance, the quality of the soil along the river, clean air and a cooler and more humid climate in the lowlands than in the highlands resulted in forage that was rich in protein. The maritime climate was also highly favourable to fruit growing, thanks to a two-kilometre stretch of land along the river where the water helps regulate the temperature.

REGIONAL BOUNTY

Thanks to their expertise, either inherited or acquired, their innovations in farming techniques, and their willingness to learn the traditional trades that support ecological or organic farming practices, the Quebec artisans of today never cease to amaze us with their creations, each more original than the next.

While drawing inspiration from the customs and traditions of yesteryear, today's artisans have set the bar higher, never thinking twice about going abroad to learn or perfect their craft.

They also know how to take advantage of the treasures of their respective regions, applying their expertise as they lovingly interpret the marvels of their delicate and precious *terroirs*.

Their talent and persistence have led to the production of a stunning array of more than 350 specialty cheeses made from the milk of cows, goats and sheep. Most of these cheeses are unique in the world, and in only a few years have earned Quebec cheese makers an enviable international reputation.

The Bois Francs area alone has 14 cheese shops that produce over 80 specialty cheeses. The area is known for its dairy farms, which account for 40% of the province's dairy production.

We also find a veritable cornucopia of fine alcoholic beverages made from raspberries, strawberries, gooseberries and cassis; wines that flaunt the expert talents of Quebec grape growers in the face of the province's somewhat rustic grape production; intoxicatingly original

artisanal beers; and game bird farms raising a variety of fowl such as ducks and geese that are used to prepare *confit* or exquisitely subtle, melt-in-the-mouth *foie gras*.

Montérégie is apple country, with the Montérégie Valley accounting for 35% of Quebec's apple production. And where there are apples, there is cider! The region produces most of the cider made in the province, not to mention Quebec's now-famous ice cider—the world cannot seem to get enough of this 100% Quebec creation.

The Lower St Lawrence region produces nearly 70% of the heavy lamb in the province, with a herd of nearly 60,000. Producers are determined to keep their artisan traditions and expertise alive.

Agneau de pré salé de l'île Verte is a relatively small farm producing fewer than 200 lambs per year. The size of the farm is dictated by its owners' concerns; keenly aware of the need to protect our agricultural heritage and maintain marshes, they know that the herd cannot be increased without running the risk of damaging the salt marshes where the animals graze.

Golden Sap and Ruby-Red Fruit

There are approximately 10,000 maple syrup producers and 7,300 maple syrup enterprises in Quebec producing

some 180,000 barrels of maple syrup a year. Quebec maple syrup accounts for more than 75% of the world's supply, and 80% of it is exported to 50 or so countries around the world.

Chaudière-Appalaches is Quebec's largest maple syrup producing region, accounting for 30% of the provincial yield. It has more than 15,275,000 taps and 3,680 enterprises, including 1,740 sugar bushes in the Beauce.

Although the Lower St Lawrence ranks second behind Chaudière-Appalaches in terms of maple syrup production, the activity accounts for only 8% of its industry and is mainly concentrated in the Témiscouata area. It has 6.5 million taps, with an average of 10,420 taps per operation. Maple syrup production has helped keep many parishes from turning into ghost towns. Today, the region has some 300 thriving businesses.

Cranberry, called *atoca* by Aboriginal peoples, is grown on a large scale in Quebec. Native to the province, both small and large cranberries grow wild here in Northern coniferous forests, bog forests, swamps, wet sands and sphagnum bogs. Commercial cranberry crops are relatively recent.

In Centre-du-Québec, especially the Bois Francs area, fields are flooded at harvesting time, causing the ruby-red fruit to float to the top, making for a spectacular sight.

Touring these regions presents a golden opportunity to discover local specialties and meet the artisans who generously offer up their treasures for the tasting.

KEEPERS OF TIME

THÉRÈSE FOURNIER was born in 1916 and lived on the family farm until she married Paul-Émile Nicole in 1942. Together, they took over his family's farm, becoming the fifth generation of Nicoles to work that land.

"When I was young, there were no tractors. Both the hay wagon and the plough we used to harvest potatoes were pulled by horses."

It is not surprising then that this stylish, cheerful and philosophical woman is still in great shape and still keeps a garden—and what a garden! Carrots, onions, turnips, leek, beets, 85 tomato plants, blueberries, gooseberries, blackcurrants... the list goes on.

"Gardening has always been my passion." In late summer, she is busy canning and making preserves. When asked whether she has help, she answers that she helps herself. She gives away the fruits of her labour since she has no interest in selling her products. And indeed, there are a lot of jars to fill to satisfy her 7 children, 16 grandchildren and 10 great-grandchildren.

Her secret recipe: work, rest and...vegetables! "It was always early to bed and early to rise... always ready for a good day's work."

Thérèse Fournier-Nicole is not interested in travelling, nor is she ready to join a senior's club. She enjoys doing what she wants to do and what she can do. She is never bored—in fact, there are simply not enough hours in a day to do everything she would like.

◆ ◆ ◆

JEAN-MARC GARIÉPY was born on the Côte de Beaupré. He has always lived on his homestead with his nine brothers and sisters. The land, where Jean-Marc raised cattle and grew crops, totals four and half leagues and has belonged to his family since 1775.

"I didn't have any particular love for the land when I was young, but our destiny was already charted for us." His love for the land came later and has grown ever since.

Jean-Marc has always liked open spaces, clean air and variety in his work: taking care of the animals, harvesting crops, cutting wood, making maple syrup. With the arrival of machinery in 1950, hay cutters were pulled by horses. The hay was then forked onto the wagon, baled by hand and tied with twisted hay.

"Women would beat the flax we grew and card and spin sheep wool. When I was a child, the sheep were tethered to keep them from squeezing through the fences that were not designed for smaller animals." To protect them from predators, Jean-Marc's father would lead the sheep onto a large rowboat in spring and take them to Île au Ruau, downstream from Île d'Orléans, where they could graze freely without fear. In November, his father would row them back home before the first snow.

At 78, Jean-Marc Gariépy remains very active and still chops his own firewood.

Could there be a more beautiful panorama than the St Lawrence River meeting the Côte de Beaupré across the narrows? You can even hear the hymns being sung at St Anne's Basilica. We are in St Famille, the oldest parish on Île d'Orléans.

The family home where **ÉDOUARDINE TURCOTTE** and her ten brothers and sisters grew up was not far from here. She was not yet 3 when her father died, and her mother passed on a year later. Despite her hardships, however, Édouardine grew to embrace life.

She met Richard Deblois in elementary school and married him in 1951. They became the thirteenth Deblois generation to farm his family's 35.6 hectares. They raised dairy cows, egg-producing hens and free-range chickens and eventually turned to crops: strawberries, raspberries, tomatoes, and more tomatoes! Picture 50,000 tomato plants!

"There were some apple trees, but they were 'horrible', although there was not much of a market then either." The couple opted for the best cultivars. "Richard paid for the last ones with the change in my purse. We were not rich, but never regretted our investment. At the time, an apple tree cost $1, but we paid only 90¢ because we were just starting up."

At 80, Édouardine is still very active. She says that she doesn't work long hours, but she goes to the orchard every day, seven days a week. It keeps her young and moving.

◆ ◆ ◆

When I visited him, **ALPHONSE BEAUDET** was getting ready to celebrate his 60th wedding anniversary with his wife Éva Lemay. It promised to be quite the party! With their ten children, their grandchildren and great-grandchildren, there was no need to invite the neighbours.

The family farm was located in the neighbouring row. Alphonse recalled that, at the time, everyone was self-sufficient. They skimmed the milk and brought the cream to the nearby butter factory.

Alphonse later worked in a lumber camp, cutting trees and floating the logs downstream. In the 1940s, he moved back to St François, where he purchased 75 acres of land and did what he knew best: raise dairy cows. At one point, he had 25 cows and grew barley and oats. He also had other farm animals, including pigs and chickens. "With 12 mouths to feed, having farm animals was practical. We always had milk, butter and eggs on hand."

Work was done by hand and the boys worked alongside their father. Although the land was fertile, the water supply was at a distance, so they dug a well and carried buckets of water all the way to the cowshed. This was a necessary chore until water was piped in. "That was quite an event!"

Alphonse Beaudet, who just celebrated his 90th birthday, is walking tall. He is a proud man, satisfied with his life's work.

◆ ◆ ◆

It was a beautiful Saturday in August and a celebration was underway on the farm in honour of **JEAN-PAUL DINEL** and his wife Doralice, who were marking their 65th wedding anniversary. The whole family was there. With their 9 children, 19 grandchildren and 9 great-grandchildren, there was no lack of atmosphere!

Their homestead in Chénéville, in the Outaouais, was acquired by Jean-Paul's great-grandfather Paul, who had come from the Lower Laurentians. Once he had cleared the land, he settled his family there in 1860. Jean-Paul Dinel was born in 1916 and represents the fourth generation of his family to have lived there.

The St André Avellin co-operative was established in 1941. First serving as an administrator, and later as president until 1965, Jean-Paul Dinel remained at the helm for seven years after the merger with the new regional co-operative. In 1969, he installed a bulk milk chilling tank on his dairy farm. He encouraged other farmers to abandon their cans by getting more for bulk milk. He also served as mayor of Chénéville, rural sector, for 29 years.

Until recently, he still operated hay-baling machines. At 88, Jean-Paul Dinel has the satisfaction of knowing he has lived a good life. He was and is happy. If he were to do it all over again, he wouldn't change a thing.

Toussaint Lavergne was granted his land by Queen Victoria and was among the first farmers to settle in Ripon, in the Outaouais region, around 1840.

GÉRALD LAVERGNE was born in St André Avellin, but moved to his homestead in 1931, becoming the fourth generation of Lavergnes to farm the land.

After acquiring his father's farm in 1946, he purchased land belonging to his aunts in 1959 and 1960. With some 400 acres of arable land, the Lavergnes operated the largest farm in northern Petite Nation, and were enterprising enough to be the first to produce ear corn in the area.

Among his various vocations, Gérald Lavergne has also operated a sugar bush. He even sold maple syrup to John Diefenbaker, who was Canada's Prime Minister at the time.

"I knew my land inside out; I knew exactly where there would be frost in the fall and spring." The three miles he walked to and from school every day had been lessons in themselves.

He married Jeanne-d'Arc Saint-Pierre, his neighbour, and they had ten children.

Gérald Lavergne passed away recently. This jack-of-all-trades excelled at much more than farming, and to his last days still worked wood like no other.

✦ ✦ ✦

PAUL DESJARDINS was born on the banks of the St Lawrence in the Kamouraska region. As a child, he dreamed of big sails. His ancestors had been navigators, but his grandfather broke tradition by purchasing some land. "We had up to 22 cows, but the land was too small, so I bought the neighbour's land. Ah yes, the neighbour was my grandfather.

"In all, there were over 200 acres, but we could not farm all of it. There were hills, the mountain, the banks…" With spring tides, water sometimes covered half the fields. Paul led a campaign to have floodgates built.

After trying to grow ear corn—which pleased racoons from all corners of Kamouraska—Paul took up horticulture, mainly gladiola, on a large scale.

Today, he cannot imagine not having a modest garden. A row of potatoes, some corn and tomatoes and gladiola, of course. In the fall, he preserves plums. In winter, he weaves baskets of red dogwood, which is picked in the fall at full moon. "My grandfather thought me how. I also make brushes and brooms."

✦ ✦ ✦

At 22 years old, **LUCIEN ST-PIERRE** started his dairy business in a village behind Rimouski, in the Lower St Lawrence. "There was a time when we had two horses and seven or eight cows. Just think that we increased to reach 200 cows!"

"We worked hard, but never on Sunday, except to milk the cows, of course. But that was not 'working'. Land was expensive too, and to clear it cost $4 an hour. A fortune!"

"Power reached us in 1942. Before that, milk was put in cans that we would lower into an iced water tub to cool before pouring it into bottles. Blocks of ice were kept in sawdust to prevent them from melting too fast. I remember the time when a quart of milk cost 6 cents. It then increased to 14 cents, and again to 18 cents."

In those days a milk farmer was also the deliveryman and Lucien had approximately 200 households to visit. Then there were the fields where oats and hay were grown.

At ninety some, Lucien believes he had a good life. "I have the feeling I have accomplished something! If I had to do it over? I would choose the same trade, but probably in a modern context."

BACKROAD TREASURES

*Come meet these artisans and sample their delectable products,
testaments to their exquisite talents*

POISSONNERIE TÉMIS

Marjorye Gingras dreamed of owning her own business, and Denis Lampron was passionate about fishing. In this area more than 20,000 lakes and rivers, their dream became a reality.

Fresh or smoked monkfish, whitefish, lake herring, sturgeon, and whitefish or sturgeon caviar—how refined! These artisans use traditional methods to process the products of their *terroir*.

FERME AUX SAVEURS DES MONTS

It took Sylvain Bertrand over twelve years to start his own chicken farm, but only 45 minutes to purchase the actual farm in Val des Monts.

The farm had been used to raise chickens between 1994 and 1998; it was now 2000. Sylvain told me that he was aware of the farm's potential and did not hesitate long. Ideally located close to the city, he thought it would be a great place for customers to come and purchase poultry while enjoying the rural setting.

Sylvain decided that he would raise only the finest free-range chickens. His beautiful birds, which run happily about the hen house, are fed a plant diet for 10 weeks until they reach the ideal weight. What makes Sylvain's chickens special is the fact that they are not given any antibiotics—no small feat! The result: beautiful, heavy, plump chickens with a marvellous flavour that recalls the way chickens used to taste, many a year ago.

Before buying his farm, Sylvain had greatly enjoyed working with Outaouais farmers. They passed on their values to him, making him want to do something more concrete and hands-on. Thanks to them, he realized that farming is more than a job for him—it is his passion.

FORMIDÉRABLE

Joanne Lévesque and Alain Charette were seeking an adventure, a way to express their creativity and simultaneously broaden their horizons.

Taking a plunge into the unknown, they started a business that would eventually distinguish itself by its unique products of only the highest quality. A reputation is not built overnight, but these producers are persistent, sharing their joys and sorrows and keeping the health of their business at heart.

Joanne and Alain turn fine, clear maple sap into top-quality confectionery. In addition to delicious classics, the couple makes an array of delectable products, all maple-flavoured: truffles, salad dressing, meringues, mustard, pepper, and peach butter. They also sell preserved pears swimming in—what else—maple syrup!

Their latest goodies are pecan pralines, which are all the rage across the province and even abroad!

Give in to temptation—indulge in some pecan pralines, melt-in-your-mouth truffles and airy meringues to tantalize your palate.

MAWANDOSEG KITIGAN ZIBI

Visitors have the opportunity to learn more about Algonquin customs and legends and indulge in Awazibi maple syrup served on traditional banik bread.

LES FROMAGIERS DE LA TABLE RONDE

In St Sophie, in the Lower Laurentians, the families of Ronald and Serge Alary have been producing organic milk for 15 years. They had all dreamed of making cheese for a long time, and the younger generation was able to make it happen, with Gabriel studying cheesemaking and getting everyone involved.

It is not surprising that the type of cheese they make was a family decision, or that their delicious farmstead blue cheese made with whole milk is called Rassembleu (a play on words in French meaning "to gather" (*rassembler*) and "blue cheese" (*bleu*). Appropriately, their business is called *Fromagiers de la Table Ronde* (Cheese makers of the Round Table). If you have the opportunity to visit the cheese shop, make sure to stock up on Rassembleu, of course, but also on their cheddar, which is available only on site, and to taste their latest, the Fou du Roy, a semi-firm washed-rind cheese made, of course, with raw organic milk.

LA VINERIE DU KILDARE

La Vinerie du Kildare produces high-quality maple-based alcoholic beverages, with names such as L'Esprit d'Érable, Grand Esprit, Marie-Chantal and Désirable. The latter is made with maple syrup and fresh cream. These are beautiful products, made by Jannick Choquette with expert care, with subtle and elegant flavours that are a delight at any time.

INTERMIEL

The magic of Intermiel will become apparent as soon as you open the door to this charming boutique and the hundreds of fancy little jars all done up in ribbons and bows come into view.

Honey, candies, juniper-flavoured dandelion-honey mustard, chocolate and honey *ganache*, and royal jelly are just a few of Intermiel's tantalizing products.

On the other side of the shop, you will find mead, nectar of the gods of Olympus.

Do you know how many bees there are in a beehive? Drop by Intermiel to learn beekeeping secrets and watch these fascinating insects in action!

LONGÈRE AU NATUREL

Longère au Naturel's onion preserves, sweetened with strawberries or maple syrup, is without question the accompaniment of choice for people with discerning palates. Prepared using traditional techniques, it is a wonderful compliment to patés, terrines, and game sausages or carpaccio.

The product was developed by Geneviève Longère, an accomplished cook. It is definitely worth making a note of Longère au Naturel's address.

LES JARDINS SAUVAGES

Jardins Sauvages' François Brouillard is an exceptional artisan who turns his harvests into gourmet meals. Wild mushrooms flavoured with sea parsley, crêpes made with cattail flour, milkweed-flower sorbet…let nature's delicacies lead you on a mouth-watering journey of discovery—indulge your senses!

DOMAINE DE L'ÎLE RONDE

And then there's Le Domaine de l'Île Ronde, on Île Ronde in the middle of the St Lawrence River. The microclimate of this island is favourable to growing grapes that produce exceptional wines. Three fortified wines—a white, a rosé and a red—are of particular interest.

BERGERIE LAVALLÉE

Twenty-two lambs came into the world the day I visited Guylaine Perron's sheep farm; 18 had been born the previous day and just as many were expected the next. While I was there, Guylaine helped one of her ewes give birth. The herd grew by some 300 sheep during that birthing period; it goes without saying that Arcott Rideau sheep are very prolific. It is not uncommon for ewes to have four or five lambs, though the average is 2.8. One hundred or so ewes give birth at three different times of year on a rotational basis.

Guylaine talks to me about her vocation, explaining that you have to be irresistibly drawn to nature to want to be with the sheep despite the inconveniences. A vocation means working without ever thinking about the day you will have to stop. It is an unconditional commitment to a profession, not for riches, but for sheer love of the work. All Guylaine ever has to do is think about a newborn lamb prancing about for the first time or the ewes waiting for her to help them give birth, and she is plunged back into her work. Her rewards go far beyond money.

FERME TOURILLI

As a child, Éric Proulx loved visiting his grandfather's dairy farm and dreamed of becoming a farmer. Working on grandpa's farm on weekends and getting up every morning at 6 a.m. to milk his 30 Alpine cows was for Éric a rich new world to discover.

Éric believes that good a cheese maker needs to be good a farmer first. Close contact with the animals—feeding them top quality hay, developing a partnership of sorts—is essential. Cows are still milked by hand at the beginning and end of the process to prevent overmilking, which makes it more comfortable for the animals and fosters trust. The end product is an excellent milk for cheesemaking. His dream has always been to open a small cheese shop and make typical French farm cheeses that were not yet available in Quebec. Today, that dream is a reality.

Éric does not like routine and luckily has a great many opportunities to add variety to his work. Above all, he enjoys milking the goats, making cheese and chatting with his customers. His traditional cheese shop will remain just that, setting the standard for Quebec goat cheese and sending down solid roots in the Portneuf community and keeping alive the authentic farming tradition.

LE CANARD AU NATUREL

Julien Dupont grew up on a farm where his mother raised poultry, although she had no ducks at the time.

One day, in the midst of plucking a chicken, Julien received a visit from a French duck farmer touring the province. Julien thought he was dreaming—he had been wanting to learn about force-feeding for a decade. When he returned from Périgord, Julien began raising mallard ducks, a more robust species better suited to the outdoors.

Julien produces the "Canard au naturel" in the beautiful, natural setting of Tewkesbury in the Jacques Cartier Valley. Toward the end of their growth period, the ducks are force-fed non-transgenic, pesticide-free corn. They yield a superb foie gras.

He says that his dream has come true and that he revels in it every day. He loves to share his cooking secrets and to be in the kitchen, remembering the times he and his brother Marc would prepare family dinners for 30 people. Today, he has a great many opportunities to forge new bonds with people and he takes advantage of every one!

CASSIS DE L'ISLE ENSORCELEUSE

The terroir of Île d'Orléans is home to the blackcurrant and its virtues. Bernard Monna is a fourth-generation liquors stillman who uses the berries he grows himself to make fine, high-quality beverages with exceptional taste and aroma.

CIDRERIE VERGER BILODEAU

Originally from the Charlevoix region, Micheline L'Heureux and her husband Benoît purchased a piece of land in the parish of St Pierre on Île d'Orléans in 1982, where they planted apples trees. Today, they have more than 3,500 trees and 15 varieties of apples.

In 1997, they tried their hand at producing a few bottles of cider, which they sold in Île d'Orléans' first cider shop.

Top quality products—butters, vinegars, mustards, jellies, syrups, etc.—are always favoured. Did you know that one apple tree can produce up to 100 kg of apples? Apples, which consist largely of water (accounting for up to 90% of its weight) makes processing an attractive option. Who can resist apple pie straight out of the oven?

The couple applies the best cultivation techniques and scouts for insects—pesticides are no longer the only tool against bugs and diseases.

If they had to do it all over again, Micheline wouldn't change very much, except for maybe getting started in the business earlier. They are grateful that they have many years left to enjoy the fruits of their labour before passing the torch on to the next generation.

LA FERME D'OC

Jean-François Émond from St Famille on Île d'Orléans did not think twice about travelling to Gers, France to learn more about raising and force-feeding geese and ducks.

His beautiful birds are raised outdoors on the wide banks of the St. Lawrence River, their health and well-being ensured by the pristine setting and beautiful scenery across from Côte de Beaupré.

Once fully grown, the birds are force-fed the best corn, in strict accordance with traditional methods, in order to produce the most delectable *foie gras* imaginable.

LES FROMAGES DE L'ISLE D'ORLÉANS

Jocelyn Labbé wanted to open a heritage interpretation centre and decided to turn his attention to the renaissance of Île d'Orléans cheese. With the help of his neighbour and friend Jacques Goulet, a microbiologist, Jocelyn orchestrated the comeback of a certain "refined" cheese. And finally, three and a half centuries after the cheese was first brought here, Île d'Orléans got its first cheese shop!

Originating in Champagne, France, the recipe for this cheese, similar to Soumaintrain, was brought to Quebec around 1635, making it the oldest North American cheese.

Jocelyn's grandmother used to make it at home, and Jacques also remembers hearing his grandmother talk about it. The recipe for this domestic cheese, which can be eaten fresh, roasted (partially dried) or refined (prolonged drying and aging for 28 days in maple boxes), was passed down from mother to daughter.

In a 17th century setting, near the Maison Drouin, the cheese shop slowly took shape. In the tasting room on the second floor, gigantic trees stretching all the way to the ceiling serve as the main pillars. It may have taken four years to build, but the wait was worth it: the shop is spectacular!

LAITERIE CHARLEVOIX

The Labbé family runs an interpretation and documentation centre where visitors can admire an assortment of antique objects (including a collection of antique tools) and learn about artisan cheesemaking. They can also taste and purchase cheeses (the aged cheddar is a must), as well as other regional products.

LES SAVEURS OUBLIÉES

In addition to a wonderful country-style menu created by Régis Hervé and Guy Thibodeau, Chef Hervé has developed some 30 exceptional products, ranging from rose and crab apple jellies to fine deli meats and other fresh products.

CIDRERIE VERGER PEDNEAULT

The magnificent apple and plum orchard of this ancestral farm yields beautiful fruit that is used to make delicious products. The pear and plum *mistelles* are wonderful examples of the owners' expertise.

FROMAGERIE PERRON

Here, history and aged cheddars have been keeping each other company for more than a century. Visit the old cheese shop and home of founder Adélard Perron. And of course, this is the perfect opportunity to stock up on cheese.

FROMAGERIE LEHMANN

The Lehmann family—Marie, Jacob and their three children—moved from Jura to Hébertville in 1983. Daughter Léa's interest sparked the family's farmstead raw milk cheese production.

Their Kénogami and Valbert cheeses are the envy of cheesemakers across the province, often garnering top prizes at national competitions. The business is now a full-fledged family affair, with all members lending their talents.

For the Lehmanns, the milk of their beautiful Brown Swiss cows is not only the main ingredient in their cheeses, it is also a source of profound satisfaction and happiness.

FROMAGERIE DES CHUTES

From the outside, St Félicien's Fromagerie des Chutes looks like a run-of-the-mill Quebec country cheese shop. In actual fact, it is an exceptional place, an establishment that reflects the owners' philosophy behind their Holstein raising and artisanal cheesemaking.

The herd has been fed an organic diet since 1978. Bouchard family members will be more than happy to introduce you to fresh cheddars, cheddars aged from six months to two years, and brick cheddars (a rarer farmstead variety). Take the time to chat and learn about the family's deep respect for farming.

LE GÉNÉRAL UPTON

On his 200-acre farm in Upton, Christian Champigny grows large-scale certified-organic crops of corn, soya, wheat, spelt wheat and triticale (a cross between wheat and rye) that eventually make their way to mills.

The most spectacular, however, is Christian's sunflower plantation, which covers vast fields. Just imagine the sight of 500,000 blooming sunflowers in early August. The seeds are pressed to make high-quality, certified-organic sunflower oil that is sold under the Champy label.

Christian and his wife Martine are great fans of old and heritage buildings and have given the village's general store, built in 1880, a new lease on life. *Le Général Upton, artisan en alimentation et maison de l'huile Champy* is a gourmet food shop where you can find organic goods and other delectable products made by local artisans and enjoy a superb homemade dessert and coffee on the terrace.

LES PRODUITS D'ANTOINE

In the Upper Richelieu, chefs who take pride in showcasing the quality products of their region expertly prepare the succulent Guinea fowl of *Les Produits d'Antoine*. Referring affectionately to the bird as the "valley princess", they are a perfect example of the partnership that needs to exist between farmers and chefs.

Richelieu Valley Guinea fowl, raised by Joanne Bourdua and Michel Lozeau in St Antoine sur Richelieu, is antibiotic-free and is fed grain grown using sustainable farming techniques on their land. The birds will be among the first to be certified by the Quebec government's department of agriculture and food.

CIDRERIE LÉO BOUTIN

At the Cidrerie Léo Boutin in Mont St Grégoire, the air is permeated by the delicious aroma of apples being slowly stewed to make apple butter or other mouth-watering delights. Denise Leclerc is an exceptional cook, and Léo Boutin is a passionate cider maker, whose ciders and other alcoholic beverages rank among the very best.

CIDRERIE MICHEL JODOIN

Rougemont's Cidrerie Michel Jodoin is quite the find! If you're up for it, hike the trails to the top of Mont Rougemont. On your way down, nothing beats stopping off at the cider shop, where you can get a look at the still, the only one of its kind in Quebec.

Top it all off with a tasting. Ah! La Fine Caroline…this may be the beginning of a life-long love affair.

APÉRI-FRUITS COMPTON

This former dairy farm is where Jean-François Prévost and Yves Cousineau began growing the berries (including cassis and blackberries) that they process today.

Their very fruity and slightly sweet fermented aperitifs are best served chilled.

DOMAINE PINNACLE

At the Domaine Pinnacle, you will find not only the subtlest award-winning ice ciders, but also the first sparkling ice cider, born from the unique combination of ideal summer growing conditions and harsh Quebec winters.

Did you know that more than 80 apples are used to make 375 ml of cider? Learn how this sweet and bubbly thirst-quencher is made from a select blend of six varieties of apples, handpicked before the first frost.

LA ROSE DE NEL

If you make you way to Stoke, you will be rewarded with the view of Bruno Girard's rose garden, with its more than 25 rose varieties.

These beautiful, organically grown flowers are used to make rose jellies, honeys and vinegars that leave the subtlest hint of rose in the mouth.

MOULIN LA PIERRE

Since 1845, the Moulin La Pierre has harnessed the power of water to saw wood, card wool and grind grain. Danièle Huberdeau and René Simard have taken up the noble profession of milling at this historic site and hospitably invite visitors in to show them how grain is ground on the silex stone.

Visitors can also purchase wheat, buckwheat, spelt wheat, rye and soya flours, all of which are certified organic. A visit to the Moulin La Pierre should not be missed!

FROMAGERIE LA BERGÈRE

Exceptional certified-organic cheeses made with sheep's milk, the Monarque and La Bergère des Appalaches are real jewels.

Arlene Fillion, sheep raiser and gracious hostess, started up this tiny cheese shop.

LA CACHE À MAXIME

This vineyard is quite a find! In addition to its wines, which reflect the flavours of the Beauce's *terroir*, the large gift shop sells the products of local artisans.

POULET BIOLOGIQUE THÉRIAULT

Michel Thériault was introduced to the world of poultry at a young age. Both his father and grandfather were farmers, and Michel decided that he wanted to get back to his roots.

To get closer to the markets, he and his spouse Valérie settled in St Apollinaire.

They bought a grain-fed chicken farm with organic farming in mind. Easier said than done, however, especially in poultry farming. Organic farming is not a money-making scheme or a trend—it is a way of life.

The buildings had to be restored and, because organic chickens love sunshine, windows needed to be installed. They also improved the chicken feed and added a tiny amount of maple syrup to the water, resulting in juicier meat and a particular flavour. As an added bonus, maple syrup is a natural antibiotic.

Michel also installed a bay window in the chicken house. It quickly becomes obvious that the 6,000 chickens on this farm are very well treated indeed.

L'AGNEAU DU GOURMET – LA BERGERIE DE TILLY

Here is an excellent opportunity to discover the authentic taste of lamb raised on sheep farms. You can buy traditional cuts of lamb, as well as smoked lamb, terrines, pizzas and numerous other delicious products.

But the main attraction at the Bergerie de Tilly is the chance to meet and chat with Denise Moisan and Pierre et Guillaume Dorion, passionate producers who are happy to talk about the way their raise their beautiful lambs.

FROMAGERIE BERGERON

Established in 1940, the Fromagerie Bergeron was the first Canadian company to specialize in Gouda. Bergeron family cheese makers gave each of their cheeses a name befitting its personality.

While the names acknowledge their roots, they also express the flights of fancy the tastes inspire!

VIN ARTISANAL LE RICANEUX

Jacques McIsaac has been growing fruit (especially raspberries) since 1979 and used the surplus of his crops to experiment with berry-based alcoholic beverages.

Testing continues, but so far Jacques has had much success with several berry alcohols, including a blackcurrant-gooseberry hybrid, likely a world first!

And where did he get his know-how? Jacques' father made alcohol, as did his grandmother. He can still remember the jars in her kitchen. She used the old recipes of the Curé Bouillon. Of course, quality control is much better today.

Jacques is proud to have his daughter Dominique at his side. Although she studied aircraft maintenance, which, he jokes, is not particularly related to the field, her knowledge of chemistry and her natural curiosity are assets. Dominique has the flair and enthusiasm needed to create new flavours. He and his daughter complement each other perfectly.

Le Ricaneux is the largest producer of berry-based alcoholic beverages in Quebec. Jacques muses that the business could have perhaps developed more quickly. But then again, every road taken serves a purpose. You have to learn to crawl before you can walk.

DONALD LACHANCE

Donald Lachance was only 12 years old when he embarked on his fishing career on "his" 20-foot boat! Of course, he had been fishing hundreds of times with his father, but this time he was the boss and even had an assistant.

Atlantic sturgeon is fished from St Vallier to Kamouraska from May 1 to June 30. Fishing resumes only on August 15, because the waters are too warm in summer. Each fish is weighed and certificates are submitted to wildlife conservation officers.

It should be noted that caviar is not the main attraction, but rather the meat of the sturgeon itself, which had virtually disappeared as a result of overfishing and chemical and cement spills, and which made a recovery around 1972.

At the time Donald bought his father's business, fishermen were catching between 85,000 lbs and 100,000 lbs of sturgeon each season. Today, quotas total approximately 25,000 lbs. In many ways, his profession is more old-school than ever.

Donald is the only one of the nine Lachance children to have become a fisherman. When he was a child, he missed more school days than fishing days. He loves what he does and would not change it for the world.

SOCIÉTÉ COOPÉRATIVE AGRICOLE DE L'ÎLE-AUX-GRUES

Christian Vinet moved to Île-aux-Grues in 1996. He had worked on dairy farms when he was an agronomy student and was trained as a cheese maker. By the time he arrived at the Société coopérative agricole, he was ready to roll up his sleeves. Today, he manages the business and is very proud of the success of its Mi-Carême, Riopelle de l'Isle, and other aged raw milk cheddars–in short, of all Île-aux-Grues cheeses.

There is an interesting story behind the Tomme de Grosse-Île, the co-op's latest cheese. Thirty-five Brown Swiss cows were brought to the island. In addition to creating a new cheese, jobs were generated and land that had been abandoned was being put to use again. The cheese reflects the *terroir's* true flavours, as the cows feed on hay cut on the island.

Christian explains that the cheese shop remains a traditional enterprise. Five of the six farms on the island form a partnership. The cheeses are always moulded by hand. He personally hopes to remain there a long time to help the cheese shop grow. More important to him than introducing new products, though, would be seeing young families settle in the area to ensure the island's economic growth–that would make his heart swell with pride.

CIDRERIE LA POMME DU SAINT-LAURENT

When you take Route 388 up to Rang Bellevue, you are rewarded with stunning scenery: 3,000 apple trees in bloom or heavy with beautiful, ripe fruit with the St Lawrence River in the background–a sight only Mother Nature could conjure! Suzanne Gagné tells me that hers is probably the last orchard of its size in this area, since the weather farther east is less favourable.

After embarking on a promising marketing career at a multinational company, Suzanne today heads the company founded by her grandfather around 1930. She brought her cider-making skills and know-how to the business and began selling her cider in 2002.

Five years ago, Suzanne set specific objectives for herself, and she has met every single one. Her parents passed on their knowledge to her and have supported her every step of the way. Words cannot describe how she feels knowing how proud they are of her.

She explains that you have to invest in order to succeed in agriculture. Farmers work with delicate products and being too ambitious can be risky. This young woman knows where she's going. If she had to do it all again, she would not change a single thing and is thrilled to be taking over the business at this stage. She wisely tells me that experience is the key to rising to the challenge and assuming responsibility.

LA SEIGNEURIE DES AULNAIES

At the mill, grain is stone-ground, just like it was long ago, and bread is baked in the outdoor oven. Baked goods and flours are available in the shop. Listen to the waterfall that powers the big wheel as you sip lemonade and indulge in a tasty treat in the café.

LE MOUTON BLANC

Rachel White simply glows with fulfilment, thanks to her profession of raising dairy ewes. In the spring of 2000, she travelled to France's Basque Country, where she lived the life of a Pyrenean shepherd, taking care of the animals, milking them in the morning and evening, and making cheese. She endured the sometimes harsh conditions of mountain life and lived in complete isolation with her herd of 500 sheep.

On her return to Quebec, she threw herself into dairy production with her spouse Pascal-André Bisson, who loves making cheese. He is also remarkably good at it. La tome du Kamouraska is of an exceptional quality.

The cheese shop is just 30 metres from the sheep barn and is built into the mountain. Its aging cellars are buried deep in the monadnock landscape, making for optimal aging conditions.

LE JARDIN DES PÈLERINS

Tomatoes, tomatoes and more tomatoes are picked when perfectly ripe and at their most delicious! The different types of lettuce used in mixed green salads and other organic vegetables are grown here by experts Andrée Deschêsnes and Anne Fortin. Pesto, herb salt and salted herbs are also available.

LA MAISON DE LA PRUNE

When visiting La Maison de la prune, stroll through one of Quebec's most fascinating orchards and admire the Damas plum trees.

Marie de Blois and Paul-Louis Martin moved here in 1974. At first, they ran their business from a shed and put up a sign on the side of the road in order to draw people into their yard. Over time, production increased, and the couple now produces several thousand jars of jam every year.

The jam is always made in very small quantities, and every batch—enough to fill five jars—is stewed over a gas flame in copper pots, encouraging the fruit to release its most delicate flavours.

FERME MARIE-ROSELAINE

Roselyne Lestage and Alain Lévesque began growing garlic after studying crop cultivation methods for this 5,000-year-old edible plant in Europe.

They moved to the area in 1997. Although some people told them that growing garlic in the Lower St Lawrence was no easy feat, they took heart in the experience they had already acquired and planted about 60 pounds of two varieties along the riverbanks. Today, they plant 1,500 pounds of garlic every year.

The garlic is simply delicious. Roselyne and Alain are unable to say how much credit should be given to the variety itself, and how much to the salt air, temperature or soil. All they know is that the garlic grown here along the banks is exceptional—the *terroir* makes all the difference!

FROMAGERIE LE DÉTOUR

Made fresh daily, specialty cheeses and a certain aged cheddar made with raw milk are definitely worth the detour. Le Détour's Clandestin, a soft, ripened, washed-rind cheese made with both cow's and sheep's milk is unique. Their latest, La Dame du lac, will certainly become popular. Other regional products are also available.

DOMAINE ACER

The Économusée of the Quebec maple industry, is located in Auclair, in the Témiscouata area. Its interpretation centre is not the only reason to travel across Lake Témiscouata, however. Indulge in a tasting, but first visit the cellars storing the Val Ambré, Charles-Aimé Robert and other exceptional alcoholic beverages, all made on the premises using traditional methods.

Vallier's father, Charles-Aimé, began harvesting sap with 200 taps in 1972. Today, with some 10,000 taps, the Domaine Acer is the largest maple alcohol maker in the province.

In 1992, Vallier became interested in maple sap fermentation, seeing it as an opportunity to give a new twist to a traditional product.

Nathalie, who moved to Quebec from Belgium in 1996, says that Vallier is passionate about the land and processing. He is in charge of the production end of the business, while she helps with developing product packaging and marketing.

RUCHER DES FRAMBOISIERS

Everything here is unique. First, there's the site: Rucher des Framboisiers is located on the banks of the salmon-rich Grande Cascapédia River near the Mi'kmaq de Maria Reserve. The exceptional microclimate is ideal for melliferous gardens.

Add to that an imposing array of fruit trees, including pear, apricot and Siberian chestnut. All of John Forest's products are also certified organic: try the willow-herb honey and star-thistle honey, both rareties, as well as the raspberry honey. They are all as delicious as they are unique.

LE PARC DES BEAUCERFS

The beautiful deer of the Parc des Beaucerfs in Rivière-au-Renard have it made. Gaétan Boulay says that in order to see the animals, you have to climb up to heaven. Thankfully, you only need to climb as high as the peninsula's plateau.

The panorama of the St Lawrence River is so breathtaking that you almost envy the deer, as they pamper themselves on a diet of flowers and seaweed.

ATKINS & FRÈRES

Here, creativity and *savoir-faire* are the hallmarks of a long-standing tradition, and regional products are *de rigueur*. Although some of the products are available elsewhere, there is nothing quite like a visit to the Atkins brothers' smokehouse in Mont Louis.

This is a golden opportunity to discover Nova lox (cold-smoked Atlantic salmon) or old-fashioned hot-smoked Atlantic salmon, hot-smoked peppercorn-flavoured mackerel, cold-smoked Gaspé scallops, or smoked trout and shrimp *rillettes*… all scrumptious delicacies.

LE FUMOIR D'ANTAN

Fabien Arseneau founded this historic smokehouse in 1940. The business then employed 1,200 persons (roughly 10% of the area's population at the time) in its 40 smoking chambers, and some 200,000 cases of herring were smoked every year.

The smokehouse was forced to shut its doors in 1978 following the closure of the herring fishery, but operations were able to resume in 1994.

Benoit Arseneau, grandson of the founder, will tell you how he is working to preserve traditional smoking methods. Recently, some 32,000 kg of herring were smoked in a large smoking chamber where the fire is made directly on the floor.

Recipes

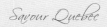
CREAM OF MUSSELS EN CROÛTE

CURRIED CREAM OF SQUASH AND APPLE

Hector Diaz, *Arôme, Hilton-Lac Leamy*

LOVAGE VERDURETTE AND YUKON GOLD POTATOES

Guy Blain, *L'Orée du Bois*

SPRING SYMPHONY

Serge Parent, *point.virgule resto & bistro, le Georgesville*

CREAM OF MUSSELS EN CROÛTE

4 servings

500 g	fresh mussels	1 pound 2 ounces
2.5 mL	butter	1/2 teaspoon
80 mL	shallots, finely chopped	1/3 cup
2.5 mL	chopped garlic	1/2 teaspoon
125 mL	white wine	1/2 cup
10 mL	chopped parsley	2 teaspoons
10	saffron pistils	
	pinch of freshly ground pepper	
125 mL	flour	1/2 cup
185 mL	cold water	3/4 cup
125 mL	35% cream	1/2 cup
500 g	puff pastry dough	1 pound 2 ounces
	glaze (egg beaten with a little milk)	

In a saucepan, melt butter and sweat shallots and garlic lightly. Moisten with wine; add parsley and saffron. Season.

Bring to a boil. Add mussels and cook covered, stirring occasionally until the shells open. Remove mussels, allow to cool and remove from their shells. Reserve.

In a bowl, whisk flour with half of the cold water until the mixture is of even consistency. Reserve.

Pour remaining water into cooking stock and add cream; bring to a boil. Gradually whisk in flour and water mixture (it is not necessary to use the whole amount). Cook over medium heat, stirring until the liquid thickens, blending smoothly. Simmer 5 to 7 minutes. Strain through a *chinois*.

Divide mussels equally and place into serving bowls. Pour liquid. Reserve.

Roll out dough and cut circles larger than top of bowls. Brush both sides of dough with glaze; cover bowls, making sure pastry is sealed outside the rim.

Bake in a preheated oven at 220°C (425°F) 15 to 20 minutes.

CURRIED CREAM OF SQUASH AND APPLE

4 servings

1/2 clove	garlic, finely chopped	
15 mL	butter	1 tablespoon
2	shallots, finely chopped	
1/2	medium onion, peeled and finely chopped	
5 mL	fresh basil	1 teaspoon
1.25 mL	fresh thyme	1/4 teaspoon
2	Golden Delicious apples, peeled and thinly sliced	
1.25 L	chicken stock	5 cups
125 mL	dry white wine	1/2 cup
1	yellow squash, peeled and diced	
5 mL	curry powder	1 teaspoon
60 mL	35% cream	1/4 cup
	salt and pepper	

In a saucepan, melt butter, add onion, garlic and shallots. Pour white wine and reduce until almost dry. Add thyme, basil and curry powder. Mix well.

Add diced squash and apples. Moisten with stock. Season and cook 10 to 15 minutes or until squash and apples are cooked. Remove from heat and allow to cool. Mix in blender, then strain through a *chinois*. Season.

Reheat and add cream before serving.

LOVAGE VERDURETTE AND YUKON GOLD POTATOES

4 servings

30 mL	butter	2 tablespoons
125 mL	celery, finely chopped	1/2 cup
250 mL	leeks, finely sliced	1 cup
1 L	chicken broth	4 cups
750 mL	Yukon gold potatoes, finely diced	3 cups
125 mL	broccoli	1/2 cup
250 mL	lovage, finely chopped*	1 cup
125 mL	35% cream	1/2 cup
	salt and pepper	

In a saucepan, melt butter. Add celery, onion and leeks. Cook 3 minutes. Moisten with broth. Add potatoes and bring to a boil. Add broccoli and lovage. Simmer approximately 15 minutes. Season.

Purée and add cream. Serve hot or cold.

* May be replaced with celery leaves or Italian parsley

SPRING SYMPHONY

4 servings

200 g	fiddleheads	7 ounces
60 mL	red onion	1/4 cup
200 g	fresh asparagus	7 ounces
500 mL	potatoes	2 cups
15 mL	wild garlic, finely chopped	1 tablespoon
30 mL	butter	2 tablespoons
1.5 L	chicken stock	6 cups
250 mL	15% country cream	1 cup
	salt and pepper	

Wash fiddleheads with care; drain. Slice onion, garlic, trim asparagus, peel potatoes. Dice vegetables.

In a saucepan, melt butter and cook vegetables lightly. Moisten with stock and bring to a boil. Reduce heat and cover. Cook about 45 minutes.

Purée in food processor. Strain through a *chinois*.

Pour into saucepan, reheat potage and incorporate cream. Season.

CORNET OF WAPITI AND BASTIDOU FROM FERME TOURILLI
YELLOW ZUCCHINI AND CHIVE TEMPURA

Pascal Cothet, Auberge La Bastide

DARIOLE OF GRIZZLY SMOKED SALMON

Mario Martel, Groupe GP

FOIE GRAS AU BEURRE AU CHARLES-AIMÉ ROBERT IN MAPLE JELLY
CRANBERRY JUICE AND VAL-AMBRÉ FROM DOMAINE ACER

Hugues Massey, Auberge du Chemin Faisant

FROMAGE À RÔTIR FROM FROMAGES DE L'ISLE D'ORLÉANS
COULIS OF CASSIS FROM SAVEURS DE L'ISLE D'ORLÉANS

Robert Bolduc, Manoir Mauvide-Genest

GOUGÈRES AU BOUQUETIN DE PORTNEUF FROM FERME TOURILLI
AND SMOKED LAMB FROM L'AGNEAU DU GOURMET

Yvon Godbout, Restaurant La Fenouillière

PAVÉ OF STURGEON FROM BATTURES-AUX-LOUPS-MARINS
IN CIDER JELLY FROM CIDRERIE LA POMME DU SAINT-LAURENT

Martin Boucher, Manoir des Érables

ORGANIC TOMATO TRILOGY FROM FERME PLEINE TERRE
PEPPERMINT CARAMEL

Vincent Morin, Restaurant Val des Sens

CORNET OF WAPITI AND BASTIDOU FROM FERME TOURILLI
YELLOW ZUCCHINI AND CHIVE TEMPURA

4 servings

CORNET

1	400 g (14 ounces) filet of wapiti	
150 g	Bastidou cheese	5 1/2 ounces
	juice of 1 lime	
30 mL	olive oil	1 tablespoon
8	green asparagus spears, blanched	
8	sweet basil leaves	
	fleur de sel and freshly ground pepper	

TEMPURA

1	egg yolk	
185 mL	ice water	3/4 cup
125 mL	buckwheat flour	1/2 cup
60 mL	sifted flour	1/4 cup
20 mL	olive oil	4 teaspoons
1	yellow zucchini	
	salt and freshly ground pepper	

Roll wapiti meat in plastic wrap and make an airtight seal. Place in the freezer for 2 hours.

Cut meat into thin slices. Set slices in a plate and drizzle lime juice first, then olive oil. Season. Macerate for a few minutes.

Cut cheese into 8 thin slices. On each slice of wapiti, place a slice of cheese, one asparagus spear and a sweet basil leaf. Roll into cones.

- TEMPURA -

In a bowl, beat the egg yolk lightly with ice water. Add buckwheat and sifted flour. Mix again. Set batter aside a few minutes.

In a sauté pan, heat oil at 175°C (340°F).

Slice zucchinis on a diagonal, season and dip into batter. Fry in hot oil until dough begins to puff up.

Remove zucchini slices with a skimmer. Strain and pat dry with paper towel.

See Ferme Tourilli page 118

DARIOLE OF GRIZZLY SMOKED SALMON

8	slices of Grizzly smoked salmon	
125 mL	Grizzly smoked shrimps	1/2 cup
30 mL	chives, finely chopped	2 tablespoons
60 mL	mayonnaise	1/4 cup
5 mL	curry powder	1 teaspoon
60 mL	lemon juice	1/4 cup
30 mL	red pepper	2 tablespoons
30 mL	corn kernels	2 tablespoons
1	shallot, finely chopped	
45 mL	olive oil	3 tablespoons
	salt and pepper	

Finely dice red pepper and blanch. Reserve.

Combine shrimps with chive, mayonnaise and curry powder. Drizzle with lemon juice. Reserve.

Combine red pepper, corn kernels and shallot in olive oil; add the remaining lemon juice. Season and reserve.

Line the bottom of 4 small cupcake moulds or ramekins with plastic wrap. Place 2 slices of smoked salmon and then the shrimp preparation. Close and chill in the refrigerator for 30 minutes.

See Grizzly page 118

FOIE GRAS AU BEURRE AU CHARLES-AIMÉ ROBERT IN MAPLE JELLY
CRANBERRY JUICE AND VAL-AMBRÉ FROM DOMAINE ACER

4 servings

1	200-g (7-ounce) lobe of duck *foie gras*	
45 mL	unsalted butter	3 tablespoons
30 mL	Charles-Aimé Robert maple port wine	2 tablespoons
30 mL	maple syrup	2 tablespoons
	salt and white pepper	
	maple jelly	

CRANBERRY JUICE

250 mL	fresh cranberries	1 cup
250 mL	sugar	1 cup
250 mL	water	1 cup
250 mL	Val-Ambré sweet wine	1 cup
1	star anise	
2 sticks	cinnamon	

Trim *foie gras* carefully. Purée the *foie gras* in a food processor until it is the consistency of butter. Add butter, maple port wine and maple syrup. Mix well. Season.

Using a piping bag, fill small ramekins and allow to cool. Store in the refrigerator. Before serving, let stand at room temperature for approximately 15 minutes. Garnish with maple jelly.

- CRANBERRY JUICE -

In a saucepan, combine water and sugar. Bring to a boil and let boil for 5 minutes. Pour syrup over cranberries, and combine remaining ingredients. Macerate at least one week in the refrigerator.

See Domaine Acer page 118

FROMAGE À RÔTIR FROM FROMAGES DE L'ISLE D'ORLÉANS
COULIS OF CASSIS FROM SAVEURS DE L'ISLE D'ORLÉANS

4 servings

4	sheets of phyllo pastry	
200 g	*fromage à rôtir*	7 ounces
60 mL	cassis	1/4 cup
125 mL	clarified butter	1/2 cup

BEURRE BLANC

350 mL	white wine	1 1/8 cup
2	minced shallots	
185 mL	35% cream	3/4 cup
45 mL	white wine vinegar	3 tablespoons
125 mL	cassis	1/2 cup
30 mL	green peppercorns	2 tablespoons
500 mL	unsalted butter	2 cups
30 mL	cassis *coulis*	2 tablespoons

With a pastry brush, brush sheets of phyllo pastry with clarified butter. Fold them in half; place cheese and cassis on sheets. Bring the corners of each sheet together to shape a monk's bag. Bake in a preheated oven at 180°C (350°F) for 15 to 20 minutes.

- BEURRE BLANC -

Pour the white wine into a saucepan, and combine shallots, cream, vinegar, cassis and peppercorns. Bring to a boil and reduce to almost dry. Whisk in butter, a small quantity at a time. Reduce.

Drizzle cassis *coulis* to garnish.

See Les Fromages de l'Isle d'Orléans page 118
See Les Saveurs de l'Isle d'Orléans page 118

GOUGÈRES AU BOUQUETIN DE PORTNEUF FROM FERME TOURILLI
AND SMOKED LAMB FROM L'AGNEAU DU GOURMET

4 servings

30 mL	red pepper	2 tablespoons
60 g	Bouquetin de Portneuf cheese	2 ounces
60 g	smoked lamb	2 ounces

PUFF PASTRY

80 mL	water	1/3 cup
30 mL	butter	2 tablespoons
125 mL	flour	1/2 cup
1 pinch	salt	
2	eggs	

Finely chop pepper, cheese and smoked lamb.

- PUFF PASTRY -

In a saucepan, pour water and add salt and butter. Bring to a boil; add flour. Leave dough to dry in the saucepan on the stovetop. Transfer to a bowl and combine with eggs. Combine first preparation with puff pastry dough.

Using a piping bag, form *gougères* on a baking sheet. Bake in a preheated oven at 180°C (350°F) for 12 to 15 minutes, until golden.

Serve warm.

See Ferme Tourilli page 118

See L'Agneau du gourmet page 118

PAVÉ OF STURGEON FROM BATTURES-AUX-LOUPS-MARINS
IN CIDER JELLY FROM CIDRERIE LA POMME DU SAINT-LAURENT

4 servings

300 g	fresh sturgeon filet	10 1/2 ounces
60 mL	carrot	1/4 cup
60 mL	rutabaga	1/4 cup
60 mL	shallot	1/4 cup
60 mL	apple	1/4 cup
60 mL	celery stick	1/4 cup
375 mL	Le Saint-Laurent cider	1 1/2 cup
30 mL	butter	2 tablespoons
3	sheets of gelatine or 1 sachet	
	cold water	
	salt and peper	

Cut sturgeon into 4 equal portions. Peel the apple. Cut vegetables and apple into a *brunoise*. Reserve.

In a sauté pan, melt butter and sweat the vegetable *brunoise*. Deglaze with the cider.

Place *pavés* in pan and poach lightly for a few minutes or until tender to the touch. Remove carefully and place in a deep dish.

Soak gelatine in cold water. Reduce the liquid to 185 mL (3/4 cup). Add gelatine and season. Pour equally over the *pavés* and refrigerate for 30 minutes before serving.

See Cidrerie La Pomme du Saint-Laurent page 118

ORGANIC TOMATO TRILOGY FROM FERME PLEINE TERRE
PEPPERMINT CARAMEL

4 servings

Appliance required: ice-cream maker

GREEN ZEBRA TOMATO CARPACCIO

2	Green Zebra tomatoes	
25 mL	balsamic vinegar	5 teaspoons
10 mL	Dijon mustard	2 teaspoons
80 mL	olive oil	1/3 cup
30 mL	minced chives, Italian parsley, sweet basil, dill	2 tablespoons
30 mL	parmesan cheese, freshly grated	2 tablespoons
	Guérande salt, freshly ground pepper	

TOMATO SORBET

500 mL	fresh tomato juice	2 cups
125 mL	sugar	1/2 cup
25 mL	glucose or corn syrup	5 teaspoons
30 mL	balsamic vinegar	2 tablespoons
	celery salt	
	freshly ground pepper	

PEPPERMINT CARAMEL

15 mL	butter	1 tablespoon
45 mL	sugar	3 tablespoons
20 mL	35% cream	4 teaspoons
15 mL	peppermint leaves, finely-chopped	1 tablespoon

TIGARELLA TOMATOES STUFFED WITH ORGANIC CUCUMBER

4	small Tigarella tomatoes	
45 mL	olive oil	3 tablespoons
20 mL	Chardonnay vinegar	4 teaspoons
125 mL	organic cucumber	1/2 cup
125 mL	organic tomato	1/2 cup
10 mL	shallot, minced	2 teaspoons
15 mL	sweet basil, minced	1 tablespoon
	salt and freshly ground pepper	

- CARPACCIO -

Wash tomatoes and cut into thin slices. In a bowl, combine balsamic vinegar, mustard and olive oil. Emulsify the vinaigrette in a blender. Add herbs and parmesan cheese. Season and reserve.

- SORBET -

In a saucepan, melt sugar and glucose in 185 mL (3/4 cup) fresh tomato juice at medium heat. Add remaining tomato juice and allow to cool. Add balsamic vinegar and season. Churn in ice-cream maker. Store in the freezer.

- CARAMEL -

Melt butter in a saucepan at medium heat. Add sugar and cook until it becomes caramel. *Décuire* the caramel with cream and reduce the heat to minimum. Add mint and stir until smooth. Reserve.

- TOMATOES TIGARELLA -

Wash tomatoes; remove top and empty. Cut peeled cucumber and peeled tomato into a *brunoise*. Reserve.

Combine olive oil and vinegar. Combine remaining ingredients to make cucumber salad. Season. Fill hollow tomatoes and place the top back on.

See Ferme Pleine Terre page 118

PEC-NORD GIANT SCALLOP CEVICHE
SAINT-SIMON OYSTER SOUP

Philippe Robitaille, *Le Monte Cristo Restaurant, Château Bonne Entente*

PRESSÉ DE FOIES BLONDS OF GUINEA FOWL FROM FERME KÉGO CAILLES
PRUNES STEWED IN PORTAGEUR FROM LE RICANEUX

Pascal Androdias, *Auberge du Faubourg*

RIOPELLE DE L'ISLE-AUX-GRUES WITH SMOKED SALMON
BERRY COULIS

Patrick Gonfond, *Café La Coureuse des Grèves*

ROGNONS DE LAPIN CONFITS IN LIGHT BOUILLON
CREAMY GOÉMON FROM FROMAGERIE DE LAVOYE

Auberge du Mange-Grenouille

STUFFED QUAILS
CRANBERRY SAUCE

Andrée Dompierre, *Maison La Crémaillère*

SNOW CRAB IN SALTED WATER
RASPBERRY VINAIGRETTE

Mario Gagnon, *Restaurant Allegro*

TROUT TARTAR FROM KENAUK FISHFARM

Les Chantignolles, Château Montebello

PEC-NORD GIANT SCALLOP CEVICHE
SAINT-SIMON OYSTER SOUP

4 servings

CEVICHE

4	live giant scallops	
45 mL	olive oil	3 tablespoons
1	shallot, finely chopped	
	lemon juice and zest	
	salt and pepper	

OYSTER SOUP

30	Saint-Simon oysters	
1	onion, finely chopped	
1	leek, white part only	
1	carrot	
15 mL	butter	1 tablespoon
185 mL	white wine	3/4 cup
250 mL	35% cream	1 cup
	salt and pepper	

AÏOLI

2	egg yolks	
185 mL	olive oil	3/4 cup
15 mL	Dijon mustard	1 tablespoon
1	clove garlic	
	lemon juice	
	salt and pepper	

Open scallops and remove top valve. Detach the muscle by sliding a knife blade under the beards. Remove small dark pouch and beards; cut the small hard muscle on the scallop side. Remove scallop and coral. Wash well. Reserve.

- CEVICHE -

In a bowl, combine oil, shallot, lemon juice and zest. Season and reserve.

- SOUP -

Mince onion, leek and carrot. Open oysters and remove flesh from the shell. Do not discard juice; reserve.

In a skillet, melt butter and sweat onion, leek and carrot lightly; do not allow vegetables to colour. Moisten with white wine and oyster juice. Reduce by half. Add cream. Reduce once again and add whole oysters. Season.

Mix and strain through a *chinois*. Return soup to saucepan. Reheat and reserve.

- AÏOLI -

In a bowl, combine egg yolks with oil, mustard, lemon juice and garlic. Season and reserve.

Spread on toasted slice of baguette bread when ready to serve.

See Pec-Nord Group page 118

PRESSÉ DE FOIES BLONDS OF GUINEA FOWL FROM FERME KÉGO CAILLES
PRUNES STEWED IN PORTAGEUR FROM LE RICANEUX

4 servings

400 g	guinea fowl livers	14 ounces
	milk	
30 mL	cognac	2 tablespoons
30 mL	Portageur fruit alcool	2 tablespoons
	salt and freshly ground pepper	

SPICED PRUNES

250 mL	pitted prunes	1 cup
250 mL	red wine	1 cup
160 mL	Portageur fruit alcool	2/3 cup
5	juniper berries	
1/2 sticks	cinnamon	
2	cloves	
10	peppercorns	
160 mL	sugar	2/3 cup

Soak livers in milk for 12 hours. Drain and trim.

Line a *terrine* mould with a sheet of baking parchment larger than the rims of the mould.

Season livers by rolling them in a cognac-Portageur-salt-pepper preparation. Place livers in mould, pour on the remaining cognac and cognac-Portageur mix and fold the sheet of paper over to cover. Cook in a *bain-marie* in a preheated oven at 120°C (250°F) for approximately 45 minutes.

Remove from oven and place a weight on top of the livers. Refrigerate for 12 hours.

- PRUNES -

In a saucepan, combine wine, Portageur, juniper berries, cinnamon, cloves, peppercorns and sugar. Bring to a boil. Let boil for 5 minutes and remove from heat. Add prunes and allow to cool. Macerate for 12 hours.

See Ferme Kégo Cailles page 118
See Le Ricaneux page 118

RIOPELLE DE L'ISLE-AUX-GRUES WITH SMOKED SALMON
BERRY COULIS

4 servings

300 g	Riopelle de l'Isle cheese	10 1/2 ounces
60 g	smoked salmon	2 ounces
125 mL	slivered almonds	1/2 cup
15 mL	sugar	1 tablespoons
30 mL	maple syrup	2 tablespoons

VINAIGRETTE

80 mL	extra virgin olive oil	1/3 cup
15 mL	balsamic vinegar	1 tablespoon
	salt and pepper	

COULIS

250 mL	strawberry and raspberry mix	1 cup
	water	

Cut cheese horizontally into two equal thicknesses. Place slices of smoked salmon on the bottom half; top with the second piece of cheese and press. Wrap in plastic wrap and refrigerate for 10 days.

In a bowl, combine almonds, sugar and maple syrup. Line a baking sheet with a sheet of baking parchment and spread almonds over it. Bake in a preheated oven at 190°C (375°F) 10 to 15 minutes, stirring often, until almonds colour. Reserve.

- VINAIGRETTE -
In a bowl, combine olive oil, balsamic vinegar, salt and pepper. Reserve.

- COULIS -
In a blender, combine fruits with a little water. Purée until it reaches a *coulis* consistency. Strain through a *chinois*. Reserve.

See Société Coopérative Agricole de l'Île-aux-Grues page 118

ROGNONS DE LAPIN CONFITS IN LIGHT BOUILLON
CREAMY GOÉMON FROM FROMAGERIE DE LAVOYE

4 servings

250 g	rabbit kidneys	9 ounces
15 mL	coarse salt	1 tablespoon
2	bay leaves	
2	cloves garlic, crushed	
250 mL	duck fat or butter	1 cup

ONION BOUILLON

250 mL	minced onion	1 cup
30 mL	butter	2 tablespoons
80 mL	Marsala wine	1/3 cup
1 sprig	savory	
1	clove garlic	
375 mL	poultry stock	1 1/2 tasse
	crushed peppercorns	

CREAMY GOÉMON

80 mL	Goémon cheese	1/3 cup
30 mL	35% cream	2 tablespoons
	salt and crushed peppercorns	
	cumin or fresh savory	

In a bowl, combine kidneys, coarse salt and garlic. Chill in the refrigerator at least 5 hours. Strain and pat dry.

In an ovenproof skillet, combine duck fat and kidneys. Place in a preheated oven at 100°C (200°F) for approximately 1 1/2 hour. Kidneys should be tender to the touch.

- BOUILLON -

In a saucepan, melt a small amount of butter and combine onions with garlic and a few crushed peppercorns. Colour lightly. Deglaze with Marsala wine; reduce by half and moisten with stock.

- GOÉMON -

Whisk cheese, add cream and herbs. Allow to cool.

See Fromagerie De Lavoye page 118

STUFFED QUAILS
CRANBERRY SAUCE

4 servings

4	boneless quails	
375 mL	cranberries	1 1/2 cup
60 mL	sugar	1/4 cup
30 mL	vegetable oil	2 tablespoons
30 mL	butter	2 tablespoons
4 + 2	fresh sage leaves	
125 mL	white wine (Riesling)	1/2 cup
125 mL	dark chicken stock	1/2 cup
	cornstarch	
	salt and pepper	

STUFFING

185 mL	bread crumbs	3/4 cup
75 mL	melted butter	1/4 cup
2	egg whites	
125 mL	cranberries	1/2 cup
	salt and pepper	

Candy cranberries in sugar and butter. Reserve.

Prepare stuffing. In a large bowl, combine bread crumbs, melted butter, egg whites and 125 mL (1/2 cup) candied cranberries. Season.

Open each quail and place 1 sage leaf and a small quantity of stuffing inside. Season. Close the quail, reshaping it into its original form.

Heat oil in a skillet. Add butter and sear quails on all sides until golden. Remove and place them in a small ovenproof sauté pan. Pack them closely so that they retain their shape. Pour wine and stock over quails and add sage. Season. Cover hermetically and bake in a preheated oven at 180°C (350°F) for 1 hour.

Once cooked, remove quails and place on a baking sheet. Deglaze the skillet with wine. Add stock, along with a small quantity of cornstarch and the remaining candied cranberries. Keep warm.

Broil quails in the oven until golden.

SNOW CRAB IN SALTED WATER
RASPBERRY VINAIGRETTE

4 servings

1 kg	crab	2 pounds, 2 ounces
2 L	water	8 cups
250 mL	sea salt	1 cup

VINAIGRETTE

125 mL	raspberry vinegar	1/2 cup
375 mL	olive oil	1 1/2 cup
1	shallot, finely chopped	
	parsley, finely chopped	
	salt and freshly ground pepper	

In a large cooking pot, pour water and add sea salt. Bring to a boil. Plunge crab into water (they do not need to be submerged). Cover and cook for 8 to 10 minutes.

Clean 8 claws to use as garnish.

- VINAIGRETTE -
Combine all ingredients and mix well. Reserve.

TROUT TARTAR FROM KENAUK FISHFARM

450 g	Kenauk smoked trout	1 pound
30 mL	red onion	2 tablespoons
15 mL	capers	1 tablespoon
2 sprigs	parsley	
15 mL	mustard	1 tablespoon
30 mL	seafood sauce	2 tablespoons
	salt and pepper	
2	lime wedges	

GARNISH

15 mL	olive oil	1 tablespoon
30 mL	diced tomatoes	2 tablespoons
1/2	bagel, thinly sliced	
1/2	avocado	
4	small bouquets of watercress	

Chop onion, capers and parsley separately.

Remove skin from trout filets. Mince trout filets and drizzle lime juice over them. Combine mustard and seafood sauce.

Halve avocado, removing stone and skin. Cut from top to bottom, making long thin slices to create the shape of a fan.

See Kenauk Fishfarm page 118

FILET DE CERF DE BOILEAU WITH PEARL ONIONS
MUSHROOM AND CELERIAC MILLE-FEUILLE

Denis Girard, *Le Baccara*

KAMOURASKA BRAISED LAMB AU JUS
CONFIT OF TOMATOES
MANDAN SQUASH FROM LA SOCIÉTÉ DES PLANTES

Yvon Robert, *Auberge La Solaillerie*

L'AGNEAU DU GOURMET EN CARRÉ
STUFFED WITH CANDIED SWEETBREADS
MAPLE JELLY GASTRIQUE

Pascal Gagnon, *Manoir de Tilly*

LAPIN EN CROÛTE WITH PLUMS
FROM LA MAISON DE LA PRUNE

Manon Lévesque, *Le Saint-Patrice*

PAVÉ OF DUCK FOIE GRAS FROM CANARD AU NATUREL
APPLE AND BLUEBERRY CHUTNEY
AND VERGER BILODEAU ICE CIDER

Jean-Luc et Frédéric Boulay, *Restaurant Le Saint-Amour*

RÔTI OF BISON FROM PARC DES BISONS
CASSIS-FLAVOURED SASKATOON BERRY JELLY
FROM SAVEURS DE L'ISLE D'ORLÉANS

Philip Rae, *Auberge Le Canard Huppé*

FILET DE CERF DE BOILEAU WITH PEARL ONIONS
MUSHROOM AND CELERIAC MILLE FEUILLE

4 servings

700 g	filet of *Cerf de Boileau*	1.5 pounds
125 mL	butter	1/2 cup
185 mL	pearl onions	3/4 cup
250 mL	celeriac	1 cup
185 mL	king mushrooms	3/4 cup
185 mL	shiitake mushrooms	3/4 cup
185 mL	oyster mushrooms	3/4 cup
1 L	game stock	4 cups
45 mL	olive oil	3 tablespoons
1 L	chicken stock	4 cups
60 mL	garlic	1/4 cup

Remove sinew from the *filet de cerf* and cut into 4 pieces.

Peel and cut celeriac into thin slices (3 mm.). Cook in chicken stock. They should remain crisp.

Slice mushrooms and sauté them once in a skillet. Drain and sauté them a second time in butter and garlic.

Sweat pearl onions in butter. Add a small quantity of game stock at the end to create a glaze. Heat the slices of celeriac in chicken stock and butter for lustre.

Put the oil and a small quantity of butter into a skillet. Sear meat. Let stand about 10 minutes before serving.

Put a layer of mushrooms followed by a layer of celeriac in a metal circle. Repeat to fill the circle.

Heat the sauce and blend in butter. Season.

See Cerf de Boileau page 118

KAMOURASKA BRAISED LAMB AU JUS
CONFIT OF TOMATOES
MANDAN SQUASH FROM LA SOCIÉTÉ DES PLANTES

4 servings

4	small lamb shanks, about 275 grams (10 ounces) each	
30 mL	butter	2 tablespoons
375 mL	carrot, celery stalk, onion, cut into a *brunoise*	1 1/2 cup
250 mL	Port wine	1 cup
1 L	lamb or veal stock	4 cups
	salt, pepper, thyme, bay leaves	
4	Mandan squash	
10 mL	butter	2 teaspoons
2	squash (other variety), diced	
250 mL	lardons	1 cup
2	shallots, finely chopped	
	salt, pepper, thyme	
4	tomatoes	
250 mL	organic olive oil	1 cup
125 mL	fresh basil and tarragon, finely chopped	1/2 cup
1	shallot, finely chopped	
	salt and pepper	

In a deep ovenproof casserole, melt butter and sauté seasoned vegetable *brunoise* until well caramelized. Deglaze with wine.

Place lamb shanks into the casserole and fill to half with stock. Cover and cook in a preheated oven at 180°C (350°F) for 2 hours. Remove lid and continue cooking, basting frequently with cooking juices, until meat comes easily off the bones. Remove from oven. Remove shanks and place casserole on stovetop. Reduce cooking juices over high heat until liquid turns syrupy. Return shanks to casserole and bathe in sauce to moisten.

- MANDAN -

Remove tops of Mandan squashes and empty them. Pour a knob of butter into a non-stick skillet and sauté diced squashes with lardons, shallots and herbs. Fill squash with this mixture. Place on a cooking sheet and bake in a preheated oven at 180°C (350°F) for about 30 minutes or until flesh is very tender. Reserve; keep warm.

- TOMATOES -

Peel and seed tomatoes. Cut into chunks and brush with olive oil. Season. Place tomatoes on baking sheet and cook in a preheated oven at 150°C (300°F) for about 30 minutes or until juice is reduced by half. Reserve; keep warm.

Pour a small amount of oil into a skillet and sweat shallots. In a bowl, mix olive oil, tomatoes, shallots, basil and tarragon.

See La Société des plantes page 118

L'AGNEAU DU GOURMET EN CARRÉ
STUFFED WITH CANDIED SWEETBREADS
MAPLE JELLY GASTRIQUE

4 servings

2	300 g (10 ½ ounce) loin of lamb	
300 g	lamb sweetbreads	10 1/2 ounces
30 mL	butter	2 tablespoons
15 mL	maple jelly	1 tablespoon
1/2	carrot, celery stalk and ¼ onion, cut into a *brunoise*	
	bouquet garni	
	white vinegar	
	salt and pepper	

GASTRIQUE

25 mL	balsamic vinegar	5 teaspoons
15 mL	maple jelly	1 tablespoon

In a bowl, soak sweetbreads in water and a trickle of vinegar overnight. The next day, rinse well under running tap water.

In a saucepan containing cold water, blanch sweetbreads with the vegetable *brunoise*. Add the *bouquet garni* and cook about 20 minutes or until sweetbreads rise to the surface. Cool the sweetbreads, trim, and cut into small pieces.

In a skillet, melt butter and combine sweetbreads with maple jelly. Sauté to caramelize. Reserve.

Using a sharp knife, trim the loin of lamb to the bones. Cut lengthwise down the centre, from one end to the other. Place sweetbreads in opening and tie the piece of meat securely together.

In an ovenproof skillet, pour oil. Sear the loin on all sides over a high heat. Cook in a preheated oven at 230°C (450°F) for 15 to 20 minutes, depending on desired doneness. Let stand a few minutes before serving.

- GASTRIQUE -

Pour balsamic vinegar and maple jelly into a saucepan and simmer until most of the liquid has evaporated.

Remove meat juices from pan and combine with *gastrique*. Season.

See l'Agneau du gourmet page 118

LAPIN EN CROÛTE WITH PLUMS FROM LA MAISON DE LA PRUNE

4 servings

1	2-kg (4 1/2-pound) rabbit	
30 mL	olive oil	2 tablespoons
30 mL	butter	2 tablespoons
30 mL	cognac	2 tablespoons
2	shallots, finely chopped	
250 mL	white wine	1 cup
1 L	brown stock or demi-glace	4 cups
250 mL	plum purée	1 cup
125 mL	35% cream	1/2 cup
1	egg yolk	
	salt and freshly ground pepper	
400 g	puff pastry	14 ounces

Using a cleaver, cut rabbit, separating thighs and shoulders. Cut carcass into 4 cm (1 1/2 inch) pieces.

Place oil and butter in a large skillet; sear rabbit over high heat, until the pieces are golden. Season. Flambé with cognac. Reserve; keep warm.

In the same skillet, sweat shallots and then moisten with white wine. Reduce until sauce turns syrupy. Add demi-glace and plum *purée*; simmer a few minutes.

Add rabbit to sauce and cook under lid for about 1 1/2 hours or until meat comes easily off the bones. Remove meat from bones and combine with sauce. Add cream. Divide into 4 equal servings in ramekins. Cover with puff pastry; brush with egg yolk and bake until golden in a preheated oven at 200°C (400°F).

See La Maison de la prune page 118

PAVÉ OF DUCK FOIE GRAS FROM CANARD AU NATUREL
APPLE AND BLUEBERRY CHUTNEY AND VERGER BILODEAU ICE CIDER

4 servings

1	400-g (14-oz) lobe of duck *foie gras*	
3	cooking apples, peeled and diced	
1	small red onion, finely chopped	
30 mL	cider vinegar	2 tablespoons
30 mL	blueberry honey	2 tablespoons
310 mL	ice cider	1 1/4 cup
60 mL	dried blueberries	1/4 cup
30 mL	butter	2 tablespoons
	fleur de sel and freshly ground pepper	

Cut lobe into 4 large slices of 100 g (3 1/2 oz) each.

In an ovenproof skillet, sear *foie gras*. Season. Cook in a preheated oven at 180°C (350ºF) for 5 minutes.

Meanwhile, in a skillet, melt a knob of butter and sauté diced apples with onion. Deglaze with vinegar, honey and a third of the ice cider. Add blueberries and simmer 5 minutes.

Reduce the remaining ice cider in a saucepan, and then melt in the remaining butter.

See Le canard au naturel page 118
See Cidrerie Verger Bilodeau page 118

RÔTI OF BISON FROM PARC DES BISONS
CASSIS-FLAVOURED SASKATOON BERRY JELLY
FROM SAVEURS DE L'ISLE D'ORLÉANS

4 servings

1	400-g (14-oz) cut of bison	
45 mL	butter	3 tablespoons

SAUCE

200 mL	red wine	3/4 cup
500 mL	game stock	2 cups
1	clove garlic, chopped	
30 mL	shallots, finely chopped	2 tablespoons

ASPARAGUS

125 g	green asparagus spears	4 1/2 ounces
60 mL	butter	1/4 cup
30 mL	shallots, finely chopped	2 tablespoons
4	leeks, white part only	
100 mL	Saskatoon berry jelly	3/8 cup
	sprig of rosemary	

Tie up the meat. In an ovenproof skillet, melt butter and sear meat on all sides. Cook in a preheated oven at 180°C (350°F) for 25 minutes. Reserve about 10 minutes.

- SAUCE -
Pour red wine into a saucepan; add garlic and shallots. Reduce to half. Add game stock. Reduce to half.

- ASPARAGUS -
In a saucepan, blanch asparagus spears in salted water. In a skillet, sauté them in butter and shallots. Roll a strip of leek around 6 asparagus spears. Reserve.

Finely chop rosemary and blend into Saskatoon berry jelly for garnish.

See Parc des Bisons page 118
See Les Saveurs de l'Isle d'Orléans page 118

APPLE BREAD PUDDING FROM
CIDRERIE LA POMME DU SAINT-LAURENT

Carole Henstridge, *Auberge La Gobichonne*

APPLES FROM LA FERME DES ANGES
AND MRS. PRICE'S MAPLE ICE CREAM

François Blais, *Restaurant Panache*

FRAISES AU POIVRE VERT AND JARRET NOIR
FROM LA CACHE À MAXIME

Christophe Busson, *La Cache à Maxime*

LEMON AND SAGE SORBET

Geneviève Longère, *Le Relais Champêtre*

MAPLE CRUNCH CAKE

Serge Parent, *point.virgule resto & bistro, le Georgesville*

RANG MISSISSIPPI MAPLE SYRUP PIE

Marc Dupont, *La Maison Ronde*

RHUBARB AND MICHA CHEESE FRENZY FROM FERME FLORALPE
IN PECAN CRUST FROM FORMIDÉRABLE

Gaëtan Tessier, *ChocoMotive*

APPLE BREAD PUDDING FROM
CIDRERIE LA POMME DU SAINT-LAURENT

4 servings

1 L	dry bread cubes	4 cups
500 mL	Cortland apples	2 cups
125 mL	raisins	1/2 cup
3	eggs	
1	tin of condensed milk	
450 mL	hot water	1 3/4 cup
60 mL	melted butter	1/4 cup
10 mL	maple port wine	2 teaspoons

RUM AND MAPLE SAUCE

60 mL	butter	1/4 cup
250 mL	brown sugar	1 cup
125 mL	35% cream	1/2 cup
30 mL	rum	2 tablespoons
5 mL	maple port wine	1 teaspoon

Peel, seed and chop apples. Reserve.

Combine bread and raisins in a large bowl. Pour into a greased ovenproof 23-cm (9-inch) square mould.

In another bowl, beat eggs, and add condensed milk, water, butter and maple port wine. Combine with first mixture. Bake in a preheated oven at 180°C (350°F) 40 to 45 minutes.

- SAUCE -

Melt butter in a medium-size skillet, stirring constantly. Add brown sugar and cream. Bring to a boil on medium heat, stirring constantly. Let boil for approximately three minutes and remove from heat. Add rum and maple port wine.

See Cidrerie La Pomme du Saint-Laurent page 118

APPLES FROM LA FERME DES ANGES
AND MRS. PRICE'S MAPLE ICE CREAM

4 servings

Appliance required: Ice-cream maker

APPLE CONFIT

4	Cortland apples	
500 mL	clarified butter	2 cups
1/2	vanilla pod	

CRUMBLE

60 mL	flour	1/4 cup
60 mL	brown sugar	1/4 cup
80 mL	slivered almonds	1/3 cup
45 mL	semi-salted butter	3 tablespoons
4	Cortland apples	
60 mL	semi-salted butter	1/4 cup
60 mL	butter	1/4 cup
250 mL	confectioners' sugar	1 cup
185 mL	crushed almonds	3/4 cup
5 mL	cornstarch	1 teaspoon
15 mL	Sortilège liqueur	1 tablespoon
1	egg	

ICE CREAM

185 mL	35% cream	3/4 cup
100 mL	milk	3/8 cup
100 mL	maple toffee	3/8 cup
3	egg yolks	
60 mL	roasted walnuts	1/4 cup

- APPLE CONFIT -

Peel and core apples carefully to retain their shape.

Use a saucepan large enough so the butter does not spill, but small enough to ensure it covers the apples. Heat butter and vanilla to 140°C (275°F) on the candy thermometer. Place apples gently in the saucepan and cook for approximately 15 minutes or until golden and tender. Remove from saucepan and serve immediately.

- CRUMBLE; 1ST GROUP OF INGREDIENTS -

Combine ingredients. Put on a baking sheet in a hot oven and bake until golden. Reserve.

- SECOND GROUP OF INGREDIENTS -

Peel and core apples; dice the flesh. In a skillet, melt butter and sauté apples until they colour slightly. Place in 4 small ovenproof ramekins.

- THIRD GROUP OF INGREDIENTS -

Combine butter (at room temperature) with dry ingredients, adding the egg last. On a baking sheet, spread a good quantity of the mixture over the apples. Add a row of crumble and bake in a preheated oven at 180°C (350°F) for 12 minutes. Serve with the apple confit and ice cream.

- ICE CREAM -

Pour cream and milk into a saucepan and mix in toffee. Bring to a boil. Simmer until the consistency is smooth.

Beat egg yolks in a large bowl. Add the hot liquid, pouring in a thin stream to prevent the egg from coagulating. Add grilled nuts. Allow to cool completely.

Churn in ice-cream maker. Store in freezer for at least 8 hours.

See Ferme des Anges page 118

FRAISES AU POIVRE VERT AND JARRET NOIR FROM LA CACHE À MAXIME

4 servings

1	basket of strawberries	
250 mL	sugar	1 cup
60 mL	water	1/4 cup
60 mL	Jarret Noir wine	1/4 cup
15 mL	green peppercorns	1 tablespoon

Cut strawberries into four or six and put them in a salad bowl. Combine sugar, water and wine. Crush peppercorns and mix together.

Chill in the refrigerator for at least three hours before serving.

See La Cache à Maxime page 118

LEMON AND SAGE SORBET

6 servings

Appliance needeed: Ice-cream maker

375 mL	sugar	1 1/2 cup
1 L	water	4 cups
60 mL	lemon juice	1/4 cup
30 mL	dry sage leaves	2 tablespoons
5 mL	egg white, beaten	1 teaspoon

Combine sugar and water in a saucepan. Bring to a boil. When syrup reaches the boiling point, remove from heat and add sage. Let steep under closed lid for 10 minutes. Allow to cool.

Combine lemon juice and egg white with the cooled syrup and churn in ice-cream maker.

MAPLE CRUNCH CAKE

8 servings

DACQUOISE

60 mL	ground hazelnuts	1/4 cup
60 mL	ground almonds	1/4 cup
125 mL	egg whites	1/2 cup
125 mL	sugar	1/2 cup
45 mL	flour	3 tablespoons

MAPLE BUTTER CREAM

300 mL	maple syrup	1 1/8 cup
4	egg yolks	
500 mL	unsalted butter	2 cups

WHITE CHOCOLATE *GANACHE*

200 g	white chocolate	7 ounces
100 mL	35% cream	3/8 cup
350 mL	Royaltine*	1 3/8 cup
45 mL	35% cream	3 tablespoons
45 mL	raspberry preserve	3 tablespoons

- DACQUOISE -

In a bowl, combine hazelnuts and almonds. Reserve.

In a bowl, combine sugar into egg whites and beat until stiff peaks form. Fold into the nut mixture.

Sift flour over the mixture and with a spatula and fold in delicately. Divide mixture equally into three 23-cm (9-inch) hinged cake pans. Bake in a preheated oven at 180°C (350°F) until golden.

- BUTTER CREAM -

In a saucepan, bring syrup to 120°C (250°F) on candy thermometer.

Beat egg yolks with a hand mixer. Gently pour hot syrup over the yolks, beating constantly, until the mixture cools. Add butter little by little, beating constantly.

- GANACHE -

Use a double-boiler to melt white chocolate with the cream. Once the mixture has melted, add Royaltine and whipped cream.

Spread raspberry preserve on a dacquoise, then spread butter cream. Spread raspberry preserve on a second dacquoise, then spread ganache. End with a dacquoise spread with raspberry preserve and butter cream.

* Can be replaced with corn flakes.

RANG MISSISSIPPI MAPLE SYRUP PIE

8 servings

	dough for 1 pie crust	
80 mL	unsalted butter	1/3 cup
80 mL	maple syrup	1/3 cup
2.5 mL	vanilla	1/2 teaspoon
250 mL	brown sugar	1 cup
1	pinch of salt	
2	eggs, beaten	
15 mL	flour	1 tablespoon

On a lightly-floured surface, roll out the dough to 2.5 mm (1/2 inches) thick. Fold and place over a 23-cm (9-inch) floured pie plate. Reserve.

In a saucepan, melt butter over medium heat. Add maple syrup, vanilla, brown sugar and salt. Blend well. Remove from heat and add eggs.

Pour the mixture into the pie crust and bake in a preheated oven at 180°C (350°F) for 18 minutes or until the crust is golden and the filling bubbles.

RHUBARB AND MICHA CHEESE FRENZY FROM FERME FLORALPE
IN PECAN CRUST FROM FORMIDÉRABLE

8 servings

PIE CRUST AND FILLING

180 mL	maple pecans from Formidérable	3/4 cup
60 mL	granulated maple sugar	1/4 cup
45 mL	melted butter	3 tablespoons
750 mL	diced rhubarb	3 cups
100 mL	sugar	1/3 cup
30 mL	cornstarch	2 tablespoons
250 g	Micha cheese	9 ounces
45 mL	sugar	3 tablespoons
2	eggs	
2,5 mL	lemon zest	1/2 teaspoon

GARNISH

5 mL	sugar	1 teaspoon
1 pinch	ground clove	

Combine ground pecans, maple sugar and melted butter. Pour into a pie shell and press firmly. Bake in a preheated oven at 190°C (375°F) for 5 minutes. Reserve.

In a saucepan, combine rhubarb, sugar and cornstarch. Cook on medium heat until mixture thickens. Reserve.

In a bowl, combine Micha cheese with sugar, eggs and zest.

Pour rhubarb mixture into the crust first, followed by the cheese mixture. Bake in a preheated oven at 190°C (375°F) for 35 minutes. Garnish with sugar and clove mixture. Refrigerate.

See Ferme Floralpe page 118
See Formidérable page 118

BACKROADS TREASURES ADDRESSES

ABITIBI-TÉMISCAMINGUE

Poissonnerie Témis
819-728-2949
www.temiscaminge.net/poissonnerietemis/

OUTAOUAIS

Ferme Aux Saveurs des Monts
883 chemin du Rang VI
Val-des-Monts
819-457-2828

Formidérable
819-827-9118
www.formiderable.com

Mawandoseg Kitigan Zibi
Maniwaki
819-449-6074
www.mawandoseg.com

LAURENTIDES

Les Fromagiers de la Table Ronde
317 route 158
Sainte-Sophie
450-530-2436
www.fromagiersdelatableronde.qc.ca

Vinerie du Kildare
274 Ste-Germaine
Oka
450-758-7371
www.vinderable.com

Intermiel
10291 rang de la Fresnière
Mirabel (Saint-Benoit)
450-258-2713 or 1-800-256-MIEL
www.intermiel.com

LANAUDIÈRE

**Longère au Naturel et
Le Relais champêtre**
398 Grande-Ligne
Saint-Alexis-de-Montcalm
450-839-2754
www.lerelaischampetre.com

Les Jardins Sauvages
450-588-5125

Domaine de l'Île Ronde
Vignoble Lafortune
Île Ronde – Saint-Sulpice
514-238-6285
www.domainedelileronde.com

QUEBEC

Bergerie Lavallée
1525 rang Saint-Achille
Saint-Ubalde (Portneuf)
418-277-2175

Ferme Tourilli
1541 rang Notre-Dame
Saint-Raymond (Portneuf)
418-337-2876
www.fermetourilli.com

Le Canard au naturel
1249 Jacques-Cartier Sud
Tewkesbury (Jacques-Cartier)
418-848-5176

QUEBEC (ÎLE D'ORLÉANS)

Cassis de l'Ile Ensorceleuse
723 chemin Royal
Saint-Pierre
418-828-1057

Cidrerie Verger Bilodeau
2200 chemin Royal
Saint-Pierre
418-828-9316
www.cidreriebilodeau.qc.ca

La ferme d'OC
4495 chemin Royal
Sainte-Famille
418-829-COIN (2646)

Les Fromages de l'Isle d'Orléans
4696 chemin Royal
Sainte-Famille
418-829-0177

CHARLEVOIX

Laiterie Charlevoix
1167 boul. Monseigneur-de-Laval
Baie Saint-Paul
418-435-2184
www.fromagescharlevoix.com

Les Saveurs Oubliées
350 rang Saint-Godefroy
Les Éboulements
418-635-9888
www.agneausaveurscharlevoix.com

Cidrerie Verger Pedneault
ÉCONOMUSÉE DE LA POMICULTURE
3384 chemin des Coudriers
Isles-aux-Coudres
418-438-2365
www.charlevoix.net/vergerpedneault/

SAGUENAY-LAC-SAINT-JEAN

Fromagerie Perron
148 Avenue Albert-Perron
Saint-Prime
418-251-4922 or 1-888-251-4922
www.museecheddar.org

Fromagerie Lehmann
291 rang Saint-Isidore
Hébertville
418-344-1414

Ferme des Chutes
2350 Saint-Eusèbe
Saint-Félicien
418-679-5609
www.fromagerie-des-chutes.qc.ca

MONTÉRÉGIE

Le Général Upton
305 rue Principale
Upton
450-549-6333

Les produits d'Antoine
2015 du Rivage
Saint-Antoine-sur-Richelieu
450-787-2988

Cidrerie Léo Boutin
710 rang de la Montagne
Mont Saint-Grégoire
450-346-3326
www.vergerboutin.com

Cidrerie Michel Jodoin
1130 Petite Caroline
Rougemont
450-469-2676

EASTERN TOWNSHIPS

Apéri-Fruits Compton
490 chemin Ives Hill
Compton
819-837-2559

Domaine Pinnacle
150 chemin Richford
Frelighsburg
450-298-1222
www.icecider.com

La Rose de Nel
1 chemin Talbot
Stoke
819-562-2440

CENTRE-DU-QUÉBEC

Moulin La Pierre
99 chemin Laurier
Norbertville
819-369-9639

Fromagerie la Bergère
134 10e Rang
Saint-Rémi-de-Tingwick
819-359-2568

CHAUDIÈRE-APPALACHES

La Cache à Maxime
265 rue Drouin
Scott
418-387-5060
www.lacacheamaxime.com

Poulet biologique Thériault
721 rang Marigot
Saint-Apollinaire
418-881-4047

L'Agneau du gourmet
La Bergerie de Tilly
4745 chemin des Plaines
Saint-Antoine-de-Tilly

Fromagerie Bergeron
3837 route Marie-Victorin
Saint-Antoine-de-Tilly
418-886-2234 or 1-800-265-9634

Le Ricaneux
5540 rang Sud-Est
Saint-Charles-de-Bellechasse
418-887-3789
www.ricaneux.com

Donald Lachance
24 rue du Bassin Nord
Montmagny
418-248-3971

Société coopérative agricole de l'Île-aux-Grues
210 chemin du Roi
Île-aux-Grues
418-248-5842

Cidrerie La Pomme du Saint-Laurent
505 chemin Bellevue Ouest
Cap-Saint-Ignace
418-246-5957

La Seigneurie des Aulnaies
525 de la Seigneurie
Saint-Roch-des-Aulnaies
418-354-2800 ou 1-877-354-2800
www.laseigneuriedesaulnaies.qc.ca.

BAS-SAINT-LAURENT

Le Mouton Blanc
176 route 230 Ouest
La Pocatière
418-856-6627

Le jardin des Pèlerins
190 route 132 Est
Saint-André-de-Kamouraska
418-493-1063

La Maison de la prune
129 route 132 Est
Saint-André-de-Kamouraska
418-493-2616

Ferme Marie-Roselaine
379 route 132 Est
L'Isle-Verte
418-898-3514

Fromagerie Le Détour
100 route Transcanadienne
Notre-Dame-du-Lac
418-899-7000

Domaine Acer
Économusée de l'érable
145 route du Vieux-Moulin
Auclair
418-899-2825
www.gitedureveur.com/fr/ext/domaineacer.php

GASPÉSIE

**Hydromel Forest
Rucher des Framboisiers**
1059 Dimock Creek
Maria
418-759-3027

Le Parc des Beaucerfs
11 de la Mary
Rivière-au-Renard
418-269-5270

Atkins & Frères
1 Chanoine-Richard
Mont-Louis
418-797-5059
www.atkinsfreres.com

ÎLES-DE-LA-MADELEINE

Le Fumoir d'Antan
Économusée du hareng fumé
027 chemin du Quai
Havre-aux-Maisons
Îles-de-la-Madeleine
418-969-4907
www.ilesdelamadeleine.com/fumoir

RECIPES INDEX

APPLE BREAD PUDDING FROM
CIDRERIE LA POMME DU SAINT-LAURENT 100

Carole Henstridge, Auberge La Gobichonne

APPLES FROM LA FERME DES ANGES
AND MRS. PRICE'S MAPLE ICE CREAM 102

François Blais, Restaurant Panache

CORNET OF WAPITI AND BASTIDOU FROM FERME TOURILLI
YELLOW ZUCCHINI AND CHIVE TEMPURA 64

Pascal Cothet, Auberge La Bastide

CREAM OF MUSSELS EN CROÛTE 58

CURRIED CREAM OF SQUASH AND APPLE 59

Hector Diaz, Arôme, Hilton-Lac Leamy

DARIOLE OF GRIZZLY SMOKED SALMON 66

Mario Martel, Groupe GP

FILET DE CERF DE BOILEAU WITH PEARL ONIONS
MUSHROOM AND CELERIAC MILLE-FEUILLE 88

Denis Girard, Le Baccara

FOIE GRAS AU BEURRE AU CHARLES-AIMÉ ROBERT IN MAPLE JELLY
CRANBERRY JUICE AND VAL-AMBRÉ FROM DOMAINE ACER 67

Hugues Massey, Auberge du Chemin Faisant

FRAISES AU POIVRE VERT AND JARRET NOIR
FROM LA CACHE À MAXIME 104

Christophe Busson, La Cache à Maxime

FROMAGE À RÔTIR FROM FROMAGES DE L'ISLE D'ORLÉANS
COULIS OF CASSIS FROM SAVEURS DE L'ISLE D'ORLÉANS 68

Robert Bolduc, Manoir Mauvide-Genest

GOUGÈRES AU BOUQUETIN DE PORTNEUF FROM FERME TOURILLI
AND SMOKED LAMB FROM L'AGNEAU DU GOURMET 70

Yvon Godbout, Restaurant La Fenouillière

KAMOURASKA BRAISED LAMB AU JUS
CONFIT OF TOMATOES
MANDAN SQUASH FROM LA SOCIÉTÉ DES PLANTES 90

Yvon Robert, Auberge La Solaillerie

L'AGNEAU DU GOURMET EN CARRÉ
STUFFRED WITH CANDIED SWEETBREADS
MAPLE JELLY GASTRIQUE 92

Pascal Gagnon, Manoir de Tilly

LAPIN EN CROÛTE WITH PLUMS
FROM LA MAISON DE LA PRUNE 94

Manon Lévesque, Le Saint-Patrice

LEMON AND SAGE SORBET 105

Geneviève Longère, Le Relais Champêtre

LOVAGE VERDURETTE AND YUKON GOLD POTATOES 60

Guy Blain, L'Orée du Bois

MAPLE CRUNCH CAKE 106

Serge Parent, point.virgule resto & bistro, le Georgesville

ORGANIC TOMATO TRILOGY FROM FERME PLEINE TERRE
PEPPERMINT CARAMEL   72

Vincent Morin, Restaurant Val des Sens

PAVÉ OF DUCK FOIE GRAS FROM CANARD AU NATUREL
APPLE AND BLUEBERRY CHUTNEY
AND VERGER BILODEAU ICE CIDER   95

Jean-Luc et Frédéric Boulay, Restaurant Le Saint-Amour

PAVÉ OF STURGEON FROM BATTURES-AUX-LOUPS-MARINS
IN CIDER JELLY FROM CIDRERIE LA POMME DU SAINT-LAURENT   71

Martin Boucher, Manoir des Érables

PEC-NORD GIANT SCALLOP CEVICHE
SAINT-SIMON OYSTER SOUP   76

Philippe Robitaille, Le Monte Cristo Restaurant, Château Bonne Entente

PRESSÉ DE FOIES BLONDS OF GUINEA FOWL
FROM FERME KÉGO CAILLES
PRUNES STEWED IN PORTAGEUR FROM LE RICANEUX   78

Pascal Androdias, Auberge du Faubourg

RANG MISSISSIPPI MAPLE SYRUP PIE   108

Marc Dupont, La Maison Ronde

RHUBARB AND MICHA CHEESE FRENZY
FROM FERME FLORALPE
IN PECAN CRUST FROM FORMIDÉRABLE   110

Gaëtan Tessier, ChocoMotive

RIOPELLE DE L'ISLE-AUX-GRUES WITH SMOKED SALMON
BERRY COULIS   80

Patrick Gonfond, Café La Coureuse des Grèves

ROGNONS DE LAPIN CONFITS IN LIGHT BOUILLON
CREAMY GOÉMON FROM FROMAGERIE DE LAVOYE   81

Auberge du Mange-Grenouille

RÔTI OF BISON FROM PARC DES BISONS
CASSIS-FLAVOURED SASKATOON BERRY JELLY
FROM SAVEURS DE L'ISLE D'ORLÉANS   96

Philip Rae, Auberge Le Canard Huppé

SPRING SYMPHONY   61

Serge Parent, point.virgule resto & bistro, le Georgesville

SNOW CRAB IN SALTED WATER
RASPBERRY VINAIGRETTE   84

Mario Gagnon, Restaurant Allegro

STUFFED QUAILS
CRANBERRY SAUCE   82

Andrée Dompierre, Maison La Crémaillère

TROUT TARTAR FROM KENAUK FISHFARM   85

Les Chantignolles, Château Montebello

SOURCES OF INGREDIENTS

Cerf de Boileau
Maison du Chevreuil
514-282-1422

Cidrerie La Pomme du Saint-Laurent
505 chemin Bellevue Ouest
Cap-Saint-Ignace
418-246-5957

Cidrerie Verger Bilodeau
2200 chemin Royal
Saint-Pierre
Île d'Orléans
418-828-9316
www.cidreriebilodeau.qc.ca

Domaine Acer
145 route du Vieux-Moulin
Auclair
418-899-2825
www.gitedureveur.com/fr/ext/domaineacer.php

Ferme des Anges
4586 chemin Royal
Sainte-Famille
Île d'Orléans
418-829-0769

Ferme Floralpe
1700 route 148
Papineauville
819-427-5700

Ferme Kégo Cailles
418-246-5012

Ferme Pleine Terre
1510 route 173 sud
Saint-Joseph (Beauce)
418-397-6837

Ferme Tourilli
1541 rang Notre-Dame
Saint-Raymond (Portneuf)
418-337-2876
www.fermetourilli.com

Formidérable
819-827-9118
www.formiderable.com

Fromagerie De Lavoye
224 route 132 Est
Sainte-Luce-sur-Mer
418-739-4116

Grizzly
418-878-8941
www.grizzly.qc.ca

Kenauk Fishfarm
1000 chemin Kenauk
Montebello
819-449-6074

L'Agneau du gourmet
La Bergerie de Tilly
4745 chemin des Plaines
Saint-Antoine-de-Tilly
418-886-4300

La Cache à Maxime
265 rue Drouin
Scott
418-387-5060
www.lacacheamaxime.com

La Maison de la prune
129 route 132 Est
Saint-André-de-Kamouraska
418-493-2616

La Société des plantes
207 rang de l'Embarras
Kamouraska
418-492-2493

Le Canard au naturel
1249 Jacques-Cartier Sud
Tewkesbury (Jacques-Cartier)
418-848-5176

Le Ricaneux
5540 rang Sud-Est
Saint-Charles-de-Bellechasse
418-887-3789
www.ricaneux.com

Les Fromages de l'Isle d'Orléans
4696 chemin Royal
Sainte-Famille
Île d'Orléans
418-829-0177

Les Saveurs de l'Isle d'Orléans
2366 chemin Royal
Saint-Jean
Île d'Orléans
418-829-0450
www.lessaveurs.ca

Parc des Bisons
156 chemin Royal
Saint-François
Île d'Orléans
418-829-1234
www.parcdesbisons.com

Pec-Nord Group
418-653-7227
www.pec-nord.com

**Société Coopérative Agricole
de l'Île-aux-Grues**
210 chemin du Roi
Île-aux-Grues
418-248-5842
www.isle-aux-grues.com

RESTAURANTS AND INNS

Arôme
Hilton Lac-Leamy
3 boulevard du Casino
Gatineau
819-790-6410
www.hiltonlacleamy.com

Auberge du Chemin Faisant
12 rue Vieux Chemin
Cabano
418-854-9342 or 1-877-954-9342
www.cheminfaisant.qc.ca

Auberge du Faubourg
280 de Gaspé Ouest
Saint-Jean-Port-Joli
418-598-6455 or 1-800-463-7045
www.aubergedufaubourg.com

Auberge du Mange Grenouille
148 rue Sainte-Cécile
Le Bic
418-736-5656
www.aubergedumangegrenouille.qc.ca

Auberge La Bastide
567 rue Saint-Joseph
Saint-Raymond
418-337-3796 or 1-877-337-3796
www.bastide.ca

Auberge La Gobichonne
51 rue du Manoir Est
Cap-Saint-Ignace
418-246-5329 ou 1-800-757-5329
www.aubergelagobichonne.com

Auberge La Solaillerie
112 rue Principale
Saint-André-de-Kamouraska
418-493-2914
www.aubergelasolaillerie.com

Auberge Le Canard Huppé
2198 chemin Royal
Saint-Laurent
Île d'Orléans
418-828-2292 or 1-800-838-2292
www.canard-huppe.com

Café La Coureuse des grèves
300 route 204
Saint-Jean-Port-Joli
418-598-9111

ChocoMotive
10 rue de la Gare
Gatineau (Masson-Angers)
www.chocomotive.ca

Groupe GP
418-687-9227
www.groupegp.com

La Cache à Maxime
265 rue Drouin
Scott
418-387-5060
www.lacacheamaxime.com

La Maison Ronde
183 rang Mississipi
Saint-Germain-de-Kamouraska
418-492-3036
www.lamaisonronde.ca

Le Baccara
Casino Lac-Leamy
1 boulevard du Casino
Gatineau
819-772-6210
www.casino-du-lac-leamy.com

Le Monte Cristo Restaurant
Château Bonne Entente
3400 chemin Sainte-Foy
Sainte-Foy
418-650-4500 or 1-800-463-4390
www.chateaubonneentente.com

Le Relais champêtre
398 Grande-Ligne
Saint-Alexis-de-Montcalm
450-839-2754
www.lerelaischampetre.com

Le Saint-Patrice
169 rue Fraser
Rivière-du-Loup
418-862-9895
www.restaurantlestpatrice.ca

Les Chantignolles
Fairmount Le Château Montebello
Montebello
819-561-8062

L'Orée du Bois
15 chemin Kingsmere
Chelsea
819-827-0332
www.oreeduboisrestaurant.com

Maison La Crémaillère
24 chemin de la Montagne
Messines
819-465-2202 or 1-877-465-2202
www.lacremaillere.qc.ca

Manoir de Tilly
3854 chemin de Tilly
Saint-Antoine-de-Tilly
418-886-2407 ou 1-888-862-6647
www.manoirdetilly.com

Manoir des Érables
220 boulevard Taché Est
Montmagny
418-248-0100 or 1-800-563-0200
www.manoirdeserables.com

Manoir Mauvide-Genest
1451 chemin Royal
Saint-Jean, Île d'Orléans
418-829-2630
www.manoirmauvidegenest.ca

point.virgule resto & bistro
Le Georgesville
300 118e Rue
Saint-Georges
418-227-7111 or 1-800-463-3003
www.georgesville.com

Restaurant Allegro
Québec Hilton
1100 boul. René-Lévesque Est
Québec
418-647-2411 or 1-800-447-2411
www.hiltonquebec.com

Restaurant Panache
Auberge Saint-Antoine
8 rue Saint-Antoine
Vieux-Québec
418-692-2211 or 1-888-692-2211
www.aubergesaintantoine.com

Restaurant La Fenouillière
3100 chemin Sainte-Foy
Sainte-Foy
418-653-3886
www.fenouilliere.com

Restaurant Le Saint-Amour
48 rue Sainte-Ursule
Vieux-Québec
418-694-0667
www.saint-amour.com

Restaurant Val-des-Sens
403 boul. JM Rousseau
Vallée-Jonction
418-253-5858